Dictionary of Debate
and Public Speaking

Dictionary of Debate and Public Speaking

Leslie Phillips

International Debate Education Association

New York, Brussels & Amsterdam

Published by
International Debate Education Association
P.O. Box 922
New York, NY 10009

This book is published with the generous support of the Open
Society Foundations.

Library of Congress Cataloging-in-Publication Data

Phillips, Leslie author.
 Dictionary of debate and public speaking / Leslie Phillips.
   pages cm
 ISBN 978-1-61770-100-9
 1. Debates and debating--Dictionaries. 2. Debates and debat-
ing--Terminology. 3. Public speaking--Dictionaries. I. Title.
 PN4181.P46 2015
 808.5303--dc23
                2015022428

Design by Kathleen Hayes

Printed in the USA

 IDEBATE Press

CONTENTS

A–Z Entries 1

Appendix: Major Debate Formats 167

   American Policy Debate 169

   British Parliamentary Debate 180

   Congressional Debate 185

   Karl Popper Debate 197

   Lincoln–Douglas Debate 205

   Mock Trial 216

      United States Mock Trial 217

      Australia and Asia 222

      United Kingdom 222

   Parliamentary Debate 224

      American Parliamentary Debate 225

      American High School Parliamentary Debate 230

      Asian Parliamentary Debate 231

      Canadian Parliamentary Debate 235

   Public Forum Debate 239

   World Schools Style Debate 251

Abbreviations & Acronyms 257

Thematic Index 259

A–Z ENTRIES

add-on (American Policy Debate)—an additional advantage to the affirmative plan; it is presented in the second constructive speech.

ad hominem—short for *argumentum ad hominem;* sometimes abbreviated as ad hom. A fallacy in which the speaker attacks the person making the argument rather than the argument itself. ("Thomas Jefferson owned slaves! We shouldn't listen to his defense of limited government.")

adjournment (Congressional Debate)—the conclusion of a debate session. A motion to adjourn is not debatable and requires a majority vote.

adjusted speaker points—the speaker point total accrued by a team after its high and low performances have been factored out. For instance, a team that is awarded 330 total speaker points over six rounds would have 220 high-low points after its high (58 points in one round) and its low (52 points in another round) are subtracted. Most tournaments prefer high-low points to total points as a means of determining awards and seeding.

ADS—*See* after-dinner speaking

advantage (American Policy Debate)—a significant improvement over the status quo that can best be achieved by the affirmative plan. An affirmative case usually presents one or more advantages. For example: "The plan will reduce the risk of famine in sub-Saharan Africa"; "the plan will increase automobile safety."

advantage counterplan (American Policy Debate)—a negative counterplan that attempts to defeat a particular affirmative advantage rather than the entirety of the case. For instance, an affirmative plan to reduce U.S. arms sales to other nations might claim to reduce the risk of war in the Middle East and also in Central Africa. The negative could offer a counterplan to increase economic development in Central Africa and claim that as a superior method of reducing regional tensions. (They would then make other kinds of arguments against the Middle East advantage.)

AFA—*See* American Forensic Association

affidavit (Mock Trial)—a statement of facts delivered under oath to a court officer and presented as written evidence during the courtroom proceeding. Affidavits preserve the testimony of persons who are unavailable to appear in court in person. In Mock Trial, affidavits are part of the case packet presented to contestants several weeks before the trial.

after-dinner speaking (ADS)—an intercollegiate competitive public address event in which speakers develop a serious point through the use of humor. After-dinner speeches should avoid mere joke-telling—the humor should be integral to the speech. The speech is memorized and rehearsed before delivery.

AGD—*See* attention device

agenda (Congressional Debate)—the order of legislation as suggested by a committee or member and voted on by the assembly. Agenda items are chosen at the beginning of the Congress from the docket (the complete packet of legislation distributed by a tournament).

agent—the subject of the resolution. If the resolution is "Resolved: The U.S. federal government should extend full diplomatic relations with Cuba," the agent is the U.S. federal government.

agent counterplan (American Policy Debate)—a negative argument that proposes that the affirmative plan should be done by a different actor. For instance, the affirmative might propose that the legislative branch of the federal government should increase investment in transportation; the negative might propose that state governments should do this instead or that a different branch of the federal government should do it.

agent specification (A-spec) (American Policy Debate)— a negative argument claiming that the affirmative must identify the specific part of the government that will initiate and supervise its plan. An affirmative team that simply says that "the plan will be done by the U.S. federal government" might be attacked with a demand for more specificity (executive branch or the legislative branch? Environmental Protection Agency or Department of Commerce?). The negative might argue that the affirmative plan cannot be properly evaluated unless the specific agent is known; the affirmative might respond that they have no specific duty to defend any agent other than the one in the resolution (the U.S. federal government).

alternative (American Policy Debate)—a component of a negative Kritik argument. An alternative may imply a course of action that differs from the affirmative plan, or it may simply present a contrary philosophical position.

alternative justification (American Policy Debate)—an affirmative strategy that presents two or more examples of the resolution rather than a unitary affirmative proposal. A standard affirmative approach to a resolution calling for an increase in federal spending on education might present a plan to increase spending on preschool programs or on bilingual education. An alternative justification strategy might offer both of those plans in one speech—and perhaps others—as independent reasons to vote affirmative. An alternative justification strategy permits the affirmative to choose just one proposal to advance in later speeches, abandoning its other justifications. Negative teams sometimes object that this strategy gives the affirmative an unfair advantage, since the negative cannot anticipate what the ultimate affirmative advocacy will be.

amendment (Congressional Debate)—a motion to make a specific change in a bill or resolution. An amendment must specify the exact words or phrases to be added, subtracted, or modified. A motion to amend is debatable and passes with a majority vote.

American Forensic Association (AFA)—an organization of college forensics educators that promotes competitive speech and debate. The American Forensic Association was founded in 1949 as a successor organization to the Association of Directors of Speech Activities. In 1966, the AFA assumed direction of the National Debate Tournament; in

1977, it began the American Forensic Association National Individual Events Tournament (IE Nationals). The AFA is also a scholarly organization; in 1964, it founded the *Journal of the American Forensic Association* (now *Argumentation and Advocacy*), the preeminent journal of forensics scholarship. Additionally, the AFA sponsors a summer conference on argumentation held each year at Alta, Utah.

American High School Parliamentary Debate—a style of debate emphasizing broad knowledge, speaking skill, and an ability to organize arguments on a topic with very limited preparation time. *See* Appendix, Parliamentary Debate

American Parliamentary Debate—an extemporaneous, generally policy-oriented form of two-person debate that values adaptation to a variety of audiences. *See* Appendix, Parliamentary Debate

American Parliamentary Debate Association (APDA)— the American Parliamentary Debate Association is the oldest intercollegiate parliamentary debating association in the United States. Approximately 50 public and private colleges and universities, mostly in the northeastern United States, compete in APDA tournaments. Generally, the topic for debate is proposed by the government team in each particular round, though occasionally the tournament announces a topic 15 minutes in advance. APDA debates, like British Parliamentary Debates, emphasize slower, more oratorical speaking intended for a general audience.

The association sanctions roughly 40 tournaments a year. APDA also holds an early-season novice tournament and an end-of-season national championship tournament (APDA Nationals).

APDA is an entirely student-run organization. Some teams have professional coaches—frequently recently retired debaters who wish to stay involved with the circuit; many coaches and judges are volunteers. Historically APDA has avoided uniform rule making and sees itself as a facilitator: it provides educational and financial support and serves as a liaison with other national and international debating organizations. Additionally, APDA attempts to coordinate tournament scheduling in an effort to minimize conflicts between weekend events.

The first APDA National Championship was held in 1982. It employs procedures different from the weekly invitational tournaments. Debating at Nationals is limited to one team per school, plus any additional teams who qualified for Nationals by reaching at least one final round at an APDA tournament. APDA nationals offers six preliminary rounds, followed by elimination rounds.

APDA debaters compete for three year-end awards: Team of the Year (TOTY), Speaker of the Year (SOTY), and Novice of the Year (NOTY). The three awards are cumulative, reflecting performance and accomplishment at sanctioned tournaments. The awards are presented at the National Championship in April.

In addition to the regular season tournaments and its own national tournament, APDA participates in or sponsors two other major tournaments. APDA and CUSID, the Canadian debate organization, cosponsor the North American Championships (NorthAms). This three-day tournament alternates each year between host schools in the United States and Canada. NorthAms usually attracts many teams from both countries. Additionally, APDA cosponsors the Worlds Championship—a British Parliamentary-style tournament that is held in a different country each year.

American Policy Debate—a format that features two-person teams debating aspects of a broad proposition of policy. *See* Appendix

analogy—the use of a comparison to illustrate a general conclusion. ("Oil is like food for our economy; a disruption in supply is fatal.") The strength of the analogy is proportional to the likeness of the terms being compared. Analogies in forensics generally serve to clarify and concretize an argument; they are most commonly used in Public Forum Debate, parliamentary formats, and the extemporaneous and oratorical individual events.

analytic argument—an appeal to reason that is not backed by specific evidence. Analytics are usually criticisms of an opposing argument—noting an opponent's logical fallacy, lack of appropriate evidence or warrant, or incomplete argument.

APDA—*See* American Parliamentary Debate Association

appeal a decision of the chair (Congressional Debate)—a motion to reverse the presiding officer's decision. Such a motion is most often presented when a member believes that the presiding officer has made a parliamentary error. An appeal is not debatable and passes with a majority vote.

a priori argument (Lincoln–Douglas Debate)—a brief claim addressing how a judge must vote, usually presented early in a constructive speech as one of several framework arguments. An a priori argument instructs a judge to look at the debate in a particular way, excluding certain types of arguments and preferring others; it says that the judge must adopt a particular guideline or procedure before considering the substance of the debate. For example: "The judge must disregard ethical arguments that are based on consequences, because consequences cannot be predicted." "The word 'ought' in the resolution implies only a moral obligation; arguments about specific policies must be disregarded."

argument—a claim supported by one or more reasons and documented by evidence. Argumentative statements emphasize credible proof and logical structure. An argument includes a claim (the bare assertion or arguable statement), data (facts, statistics, or expert opinion that support the claim), and a warrant (a logical connection between the data and the claim). *See also* Toulmin model

argument from authority—a fallacy in which the position or reputation of a person or organization is mistakenly substituted for evidence or warrants. ("Gen. Colin Powell says that we need to keep our forces in Afghanistan until 2016." "Why must we do that?" "Because General Powell says so.")

argument preference—an intellectual or stylistic bias held by a debate judge. Some judges might frown on counterintuitive arguments; others might insist on expert evidence rather than support through analogy or pure logic; still others might tend to disregard arguments about definitions or rules. Debaters and coaches will consider known argument preferences in deciding which judges they might strike or prefer.

artificial competition—a counterplan is artificially competitive if its text simply bans or prohibits all or part of the affirmative proposal without testing the central idea of that proposal. Consider an affirmative proposal that increases agricultural subsidies. A counterplan that captures the funding for the affirmative plan and uses it to fund AIDS research would be technically mutually exclusive with the plan, since it is not possible to spend the same money twice. Because the counterplan gives no reason why spending money on AIDS research is a reason to reject spending money on agricultural subsidies, the counterplan is not truly competitive. Almost all judges regard artificial competition as an illegitimate tactic.

Asian Parliamentary Debate (Asians)—a Parliamentary format that involves two three-person teams who are assigned the side they will debate. It is the predominant high school and college debate format in Australia and in many Asian countries. *See* Appendix, Parliamentary Debate

A-spec—*See* agent specification

assertion—an unsupported statement; a conclusion that lacks evidence for support. Some types of debate may accept intuitive assertions on face; others, especially policy and Lincoln–Douglas debate, reject most claims that are unsupported by statistics or expert opinion.

attention device—a brief anecdote, quotation, or joke presented at the beginning of an extemporaneous or prepared speech. A good attention device amuses or piques the curiosity of the audience and provides a suitable link to the theme of the speech. ("When we consider foreign policy and the uses of diplomacy, there is no shortage of great men who have attempted to guide us: Machiavelli, Lord Acton, Winston Churchill, Henry Kissinger. Today, though, I'd like to consider the words of a different kind of expert, Al Capone, who once said: 'You can get a lot farther with a kind word and a gun than with a kind word alone.' This brings me to today's question: 'What can the United States do to solve the Syrian crisis?'") An attention device is sometimes called an "attention-getting device," or AGD.

attitudinal inherency (American Policy Debate)—a preference or sentiment in the present system that prevents an agreement on a solution to a problem. An affirmative team attempting to reduce air pollution might cite Americans' preference for automobiles over mass transit as an attitude that, absent the plan, will ensure high levels of pollution. (The plan might seek to change this preference by significantly raising gasoline taxes or by imposing financial penalties for driving in central cities.)

audience adaptation—changing a speech to fit the characteristics and needs of an audience. Speakers might consider their audience's age, gender, professional or educational background, and known or suspected biases, as well as the audience's familiarity with the issue. In most forensics events, determining which style of speaking would make the audience most comfortable is also critical. A group of community judges who are unfamiliar with forensics, for instance, would require a slower rate of speech and a variety of rhetorical appeals, with more analogies and examples, than experienced judges.

Aunt Sally—*See* straw man

authorship speech (Congressional Debate)—the opening speech urging passage of a bill or resolution, delivered by the author of that resolution. An authorship speech is called a "sponsorship speech" if given by a student who is not affiliated with the school that presented the legislation. Author or sponsorship speeches are followed by a 2-minute questioning period.

B

backflowing (American Policy Debate)—taking notes on a partner's constructive speech. Frequently, the second negative speaker will compile notes on what the first negative constructive has said, so that the first negative has a proper record to consult during rebuttals. Similarly, the first affirmative constructive speaker will backflow the second affirmative constructive.

back-tabbing (Worlds University Debate)—a process by which debaters try to work out the results during closed adjudication rounds. Teams with similar records meet each other in later rounds; debaters will infer from those pairings (and from inadvertently disclosed or leaked decisions) who has won and lost previous rounds.

ballot—the document a judge uses to record her decision or rankings in a debate or speech round. At minimum, a ballot will contain a judge's decision (e.g., affirmative or negative, pro or con, first through sixth ranks in a speech contest) and speaker points assigned to each contestant. Many ballots have room for the judge to write additional comments. Some tournaments now use online ballots and other forms of electronic tabulation rather than paper ballots.

begging the question—a fallacy in which a proposition requiring proof is assumed without proof; an argument that takes for granted what it is supposed to prove. A debater who claims that "Marijuana use is very harmful.

If it were not very harmful, it would not be illegal," "begs the question" of whether illegality is proof of a harm. Another type of question begging might involve the use of an undefined general term: "Capitalism is good because it promotes rational self-interest" begs the question of what "rational" might mean in this context.

best definition standard (American Policy Debate)—a negative topicality argument. The negative might argue that the judge must use the best definition of a word or phrase offered in the round (not merely an acceptable definition) to decide whether the plan is topical. For instance, an affirmative team might cite a broad definition of "national security" as "that which protects America"; a negative team might insist on a more precise definition from a foreign affairs expert or some definition that itemizes necessary conditions for national security. Affirmatives often argue that there is no need to choose a "best" definition—that a definition need only be reasonable and that no suitable way to determine a "best" definition exists.

bias—a predisposition that prevents a fair, balanced judgment. Debaters often challenge an opponent's evidence if they believe that the source is biased. Bias may result from self-interest (a teachers' union is, of course, very likely to favor higher teacher salaries and larger school budgets; government officials will generally defend the policies they have enacted) or from consistent identification with a particular ideology (the Cato Institute, for instance, almost always advocates for smaller government).

big picture—an attempt to provide the judge with a clear, synthetic summary of the major issues in a debate round as opposed to discussing each argument individually. For example: "You can grant every one of my opponent's arguments and still vote for me. He argues only that my plan will cause harm to the economy. I argue that, without my plan, tens of thousands of people will die." Teams generally present "big picture" statements in the last rebuttal.

bill (Congressional Debate)—a legislative proposal that becomes law if passed. Bills in Congressional Debate must have national jurisdiction. A bill is typically divided into sections. The first section is a brief statement of action; subsequent sections indicate details, including how the bill will be funded (if necessary), the mechanism of enforcement, and the date on which the bill will take effect. Congressional Debate draws a distinction between a bill and a resolution, which states a position or calls on another body for action but does not itself propose action by the Congress.

blank slate judging (American Policy Debate)—a blank slate judge sets aside any previous knowledge or bias regarding the topic and reaches a decision based solely on the information and arguments the debaters provide, accepting an argument as valid until it is refuted. Blank slate judging might be contrasted with critic-of-argument judging, which may reject insufficiently warranted claims, or with skills judging, which focuses on presentation more than on argument.

block—a prepared set of arguments relating to a single point. The content of blocks varies with the format. For instance, American Policy and Lincoln–Douglas blocks would include mostly quoted evidence from experts; Parliamentary blocks or briefs might favor paraphrases of sources, examples, and analogies. Debaters prepare by brainstorming or anticipating likely opposing arguments and creating blocks that answer them.

block (American Policy Debate)—the second negative constructive speech and the first negative rebuttal considered together as a single 12- or 15-minute block of time ("They really expanded a lot of arguments in their block.").

blow up (American Policy Debate)—to greatly expand an initial argument in subsequent speeches. For instance, a negative team might present a disadvantage in the first negative constructive. The second negative speaker might provide multiple responses to each of the affirmative responses to the disadvantage, might also provide additional impacts to the disadvantage or indicate additional links between the plan and the disadvantage.

bracket—the standard system of organizing elimination rounds. For example, a tournament might clear the top 16 teams into elimination rounds based on their win-loss records and speaker points. A standard bracket would pair the top-seeded team from preliminary rounds against the sixteenth seed, the second seed against the fifteenth, and so on until all teams are paired. If a lower-seeded team defeats the higher seed, it assumes the higher seeded team's place in the bracket.

brainstorming—a group discussion intended to generate ideas; one step in the analysis of a debate resolution. First attempts at brainstorming are usually open and inclusive, asking debaters to generate any and all possible arguments or approaches. A coach or group leader later attempts to select and synthesize the most promising approaches.

breaking brackets—a variation on a normal elimination round pairing in which tournament officials will adjust the usual pairing schema to prevent contestants from debating other contestants from their school. For example, if the first and sixteenth seeds in an octafinal bracket are from the same school, the tabulation staff might adjust the pairing, pitting the first seed against the fifteenth and the second seed against the sixteenth.

break round—a preliminary debate that determines whether contestants will advance to elimination rounds. If a tournament requires a record of four wins and two losses to advance, and two teams who each have three wins and two losses debate each other, that round is a "break round."

brink (American Policy Debate)—the threshold of a large, catastrophic impact event; a key component of any disadvantage argument. For instance, a negative team might argue that the United States is not yet in an economic depression, but is nearly so and that action advocated by the affirmative would push the nation into a disaster. In short, the United States is on the *brink* of an enormous impact. The affirmative might respond that we are not near the brink or that the tipping point identified by the negative has already been passed, yet no disaster has occurred.

British Parliamentary Debate (BP)—a parliamentary debate format that calls for four teams of two speakers each—two teams for the Government and two for the Opposition. Teams compete both against the other side of the House and the other team on their side. *See* Appendix

burden of proof—generally, the requirement to provide evidence in support of claims; more specifically, an affirmative team's duty to provide evidence proving that the resolution is true.

burden of rebuttal—*See* burden of rejoinder

burden of rejoinder—an opponent's obligation to respond to the affirmative case with warranted arguments; sometimes called "burden of rebuttal."

business confidence disadvantage (American Policy Debate)—a negative argument claiming that an economic change embedded in the affirmative proposal will cause businesspeople and investors to lose confidence in the U.S. economy. For instance, the affirmative might increase environmental regulation; complying with these regulations would be a sudden and unanticipated expense for industry, which, in turn, would create uncertainty in economic forecasts. Businesses would be less likely to expand and investors would be less likely to provide capital, thus creating an economic downturn.

bye—a round in which one or more contestants or teams do not compete. Typically a single bye may be given in a preliminary round if the tournament has an odd number of entries. Byes may be chosen at random; in later preliminary rounds, tournaments often allocate a bye to a winless team. In the first elimination round, byes may also be given to high-seeded teams. A bye round is recorded as a win. Debaters who receive a bye in a preliminary round are awarded the average of their speaker points from other rounds.

call to order (Congressional Debate)—the announcement that a session is about to begin; usually spoken by the presiding officer.

Canadian Parliamentary Debate—an impromptu style, involving two teams of two debaters, that emphasizes argumentation and rhetoric rather than in-depth research. *See* Appendix, Parliamentary Debate

Canadian University Society for Intercollegiate Debate (CUSID)—a national student-run organization that governs all competitive university debating and public speaking in Canada. American teams from the state of Alaska also compete in CUSID-sponsored competitions. CUSID sanctions a number of tournaments each year, including the Canadian National Debating Championship and the Canadian National French Debating Championship, and cosponsors the North American Debating Championship with the American Parliamentary Debate Association. CUSID also sponsors Canadian participation in international contests. Additionally CUSID coordinates communication between member schools, notably through the online forum CUSIDnet, which is the world's first online student debating forum.

CUSID is subdivided into three regional bodies that represent different regions of Canada: CUSID East, for the Atlantic Provinces; CUSID West, for the Western Provinces, the Territories, and Alaska; and CUSID Central, for Ontario and Quebec. Each region conducts its own championship tournament.

card (American Policy Debate)—a quotation from published material presented in support of an argument. ("This card tells you that China's economic influence in Africa is increasing."; "May I see your Krugman card?") Before the introduction of personal computers, debaters assembled evidence on 4 x 6 inch note cards organized in boxes or drawers that they carried to contests. *See also* evidence, piece of

case—a debate team's basic position on the resolution, consisting of the initial arguments that the team presents in support of that position. In American Policy Debate, only the affirmative team presents a case; in Lincoln–Douglas and Public Forum debate, the negative team also presents a case. Commonly, a case consists of one or more major arguments, which may be referred to as "contentions," "advantages," or "observations," and which contain claims supported by evidence.

case packet (Mock Trial)—material provided to Mock Trial teams several weeks before the competition. A case packet typically contains: the rules and procedures of competition, the facts of the case, a list of stipulations both sides have agreed to, witnesses and exhibits, copies of affidavits, jury instructions, and copies of statutes that apply to the case at hand.

case side (American Policy Debate)—the portion of the debate devoted to arguments on harm, significance, inherency, and solvency, as opposed to topicality, disadvantages, counterplans, and Kritiks (sometimes known as "plan side").

causation—a relationship between two phenomena in which one is demonstrated to cause the other. Debaters distinguish causation from correlation, which merely identifies a relationship. For example, a debater may observe that children with low reading scores often attend poorly funded schools; however, that is insufficient to prove that a lack of funding *causes* low performance. On the other hand, studies showing that poorly funded schools lack the money to hire tutors and remedial teachers would establish a causal link.

CEDA—*See* Cross Examination Debate Association

chair—the lead judge on an elimination round panel. In addition to casting a ballot, the chair is usually responsible for getting the round started on time, maintaining order in the contest room, and returning ballots to the tabulation room.

chamber (Congressional Debate)—one of the two divisions of the legislature; typically, the House of Representatives and the Senate. The term also denotes the subdivisions of the House and Senate; most student Congresses divide contestants into rooms of 15–20 contestants. Some competitions hold two or three sessions for all students, and then conclude by giving awards to the best speakers in each chamber; others advance the highest-scoring students in their chambers to quarterfinal or semifinal elimination rounds.

Chamber Debate (Parliamentary Debate)—a modified form of Parliamentary Debate often found in Asia and Australia. Chamber Debate uses four-person, rather than three-person, teams; the additional debater does not speak but conducts electronic research during the round.

chief adjudicator (Worlds University Debate)—the individual who oversees the organization of debates at a tournament.

children's literature (Individual Events)—a competitive event in which a student presents material designed to be read to young children. The selection, which can be no longer than 10 minutes, including the introduction, must be from a single published fiction or non-fiction piece, play, a single long poem, or a program of poetry. The student may use vocal skills, facial expressions, and/or hand gestures to develop a narrator and character/s.

circular reasoning—a fallacy in which a premise depends solely on, or essentially restates, the conclusion. "You can't give me a bad grade; I always get good grades" is circular; it has omitted one or more premises (in this case, "I am an excellent student; excellent students always get good grades."). "Sandy's the best teacher in our department because—well, because she's the finest teacher" is circular; it simply rewords the original claim.

circumvention argument (American Policy Debate)—a type of negative solvency argument that claims that actors opposed to the affirmative plan will subvert its intention, or "get around," the plan. Generally, a circumvention argument consists of motive (reasons why people oppose the plan) and mechanism (a method of acting on the motive). Consider an affirmative proposal to increase racial equity in employment. A circumvention argument might claim that a significant number of employers are strongly opposed to the plan and that they can successfully evade plan enforcement by masking their racist employment policies.

citation—a complete account of the source of quoted material, including the author and his or her qualifications, the title of the book or article, the date of publication, the URL, and the page numbers, where applicable. At many tournaments, the debater reads only the author and year, but will provide the full citation on request. *See also* evidence, piece of

cite—*See* citation

claim—an arguable statement. In debate, a claim is distinct from any supporting evidence or reasoning; it is simply an assertion. Claims can be divided into claims of fact (to state that something is or is not objectively true); claims of value (to assert that something is good or bad, absolutely or comparatively); and claims of policy (to state that one course of action is superior to another).

clash—direct refutation of an opposing argument. Speeches that refer to the specific arguments presented by an opponent and answer those arguments with reasoning and evidence are providing good clash. Speeches that simply repeat a partner's claims, or answer opponents selectively or generally, are said to be deficient in clash.

closed adjudication (Worlds Format Debate)—a policy forbidding judges from disclosing decisions or making comments after a debate round. Results at closed adjudication tournaments are not made public until the tournament has concluded.

closed cross-examination (American Policy Debate)— a cross-examination period in which only the questioner and the respondent participate—without assistance or commentary from their partners.

closed-ended question—a question that directs the respondent to a limited range of answers ("When was the last time that the United States had a budget surplus?" "Which piece of evidence in your speech proves that the Chinese will dislike the affirmative plan?") Closed-end questions are designed to prevent a respondent from wasting time; they may be used to compel an opponent to commit to a particular rather than a general advocacy or to demonstrate vagueness or absence of evidence to the judge.

closeout—*See* walkover

closing argument (Mock Trial)—the last speech given by each side; contains a summary of their most compelling arguments.

comedy case (Parliamentary Debate)—In Parliamentary Debate, a deliberately frivolous debate topic. "Disneyland should secede from the United States" or "The Social Security system should be transformed into a free buffet" are examples. When debating this type of case, the round often becomes a contest of wit and style rather than pure analysis.

committee (Congressional Debate)—a subset of a legislative body devoted to a specific task or range of issues. The usual functions of committees are to edit legislation and to produce an agenda from bills and resolutions submitted by competing schools.

committee of the whole (Congressional Debate)—an entire chamber of Congress meeting as a committee under more relaxed rules of debate and discussion that permit a more spontaneous flow of conversation.

communication analysis (Individual Events)—an original, analytical speech that offers an explanation and/or evaluation of a communication event (such as a speech, speaker, movement, poem, poster, film, or campaign) through the use of rhetorical devices. Audio-visual aids may be used to supplement and reinforce the message. The speech need not be memorized; the maximum length is 10 minutes. Communication analysis is offered at college Individual Events tournaments sponsored by the American Forensic Association; it is similar to rhetorical criticism offered at tournaments sponsored by the National Forensic Association.

community judge—a judge with no background in competitive debate recruited from the community that is hosting the tournament. Community-judged tournaments direct the debaters toward more straightforward, "common person" means of persuasion through the use of emotional appeals, examples, and analogies. Such tournaments are frequently designed to build local awareness of a school's debate program.

community preferences—a method of assigning judges to rounds. Prior to the tournament, each team is allowed to rank the available judges. The judges most preferred by tournament contestants are then assigned to judge crucial rounds, while less-preferred judges receive less important assignments.

comparative advantage (American Policy Debate)—the predominant type of case construction in policy debate. The affirmative team argues that its proposal will be beneficial compared with the present system. This is distinct from a stock issues model—in which the affirmative identifies a problem and attempts to solve it in its entirety.

competing interpretations (American Policy Debate)—a standard for judging the acceptability of definitions. For instance, an affirmative team might define "significant" as "more than 20%," while the negative might define the word as "having a substantial effect." In objecting to the affirmative definition, the negative team might argue that the judge must choose the better of the two definitions. The competing interpretations standard is distinct from the reasonability standard, often favored by the affirmative, under which the judge might accept any reasonable definition of a word. These standards are presented as part of a topicality argument (negative) or defense against a topicality argument (affirmative).

conditional argument (American Policy Debate)—an argument whose validity depends on the truth of some preceding argument. "If it is sunny tomorrow, we should go to the beach" is a conditional argument; "we should go to the beach" only under certain circumstances. In policy and Lincoln–Douglas debate, conditional arguments allow negative teams to present a variety of reasons to reject the affirmative proposal ("There is no problem; if there were, the plan would not solve the problem; if it did solve the problem, it would create worse problems."). Conditionality is often the premise of negative counterplans ("If we want to expand public transportation, we should have state and local governments do it, rather than the federal government.") or Kritiks ("If the affirmative plan entrenches capitalism, we should reject it."). Some judges object to conditional arguments, and affirmative teams may argue that conditionality is an unacceptable tactic.

conditionality—*See* conditional argument

Congressional Debate—a form of debate in which students emulate members of the U.S. Congress by debating bills and resolutions. *See* Appendix

Congressional questioning period (Congressional Debate)—a period following each speech in which Congressional debaters may question the speaker. Each debater is recognized in turn by the presiding officer and may ask a single question. Time limits on questioning vary from league to league.

con speech (Congressional Debate)—the initial speech opposing a bill or resolution, often followed by a question period.

constraint—in the context of persuasion, an event, person, object, or relation that might limit a speaker's choice of arguments or appeals. An audience made impatient by a schedule delay might effectively limit the amount of time available to the speaker; a speech on abortion will make different argument choices for an audience of young women than it would for an older Roman Catholic audience.

constructive speech—an early speech devoted to presentation of a team's fundamental position. In policy and Lincoln–Douglas debate, the first affirmative constructive is the only completely pre-written speech in a debate round. After constructive speeches have concluded, no new lines of argument may be introduced.

consultation counterplan (American Policy Debate)—a counterplan in which the negative proposes that the core of the affirmative proposal should be adopted, but only after consultation with some third party, usually another government or an international organization. Consultation counterplans are generally presented against foreign policy proposals; they claim that action without consultation would injure U.S. relations with other international actors, thereby increasing the risk of an economic downturn or war.

con team (Public Forum Debate)—the negative team in a Public Forum round; its job is to prove the resolution untrue.

contention—a major, substantive argument in a prepared affirmative or negative case. Typically cases include one to four contentions supported by reasoning and evidence. The contentions are sometimes subdivided ("Contention III. U.S. military presence in East Asia creates regional stability" might be subdivided into "A. South Korea" and "B. Taiwan.").

correlation—a statistical relationship between two phenomena that may suggest, but does not prove, causation. For instance, I may observe that people who wear jeans are happier than those who do not; but I may not immediately conclude that jeans are a cause of happiness. Additionally, correlation does not necessarily suggest the direction of causation; it may be that happiness causes people to wear jeans rather than the reverse.

counter-case (Parliamentary Debate)—a policy proposal presented by the Opposition. A counter-case is a Parliamentary version of a policy debate counterplan and has similar features. It should not simply be a statement of the status quo, and it must be competitive with (a reason to reject) the Government's proposal. For instance, if the Government proposes U.S. government action to reduce ocean pollution, the opposition might propose a multi-national approach as a superior solution. Counter-cases are generally restricted to National Parliamentary Debate Association debates.

counter-model (Parliamentary Debate)—in Australia-Asia Debate, a proposal offered by the negative, or opposition, team.

counteropp (Worlds Format Debate)—a specific alternative proposal presented by the opening Opposition speaker. For example, the Government might propose that schools require drug testing for all teachers; the Opposition might present a counteropp that increases counseling and rehabilitation support for teachers.

counterplan (American Policy Debate, Parliamentary Debate)—a negative strategy admitting a need for change but offering a plan or solution that differs from the affirmative proposal. Traditionally, the counterplan is presented in the first negative constructive speech. To win, a counterplan must be competitive (a reason to reject the affirmative proposal), superior to the affirmative plan in the areas it addresses, and less disadvantageous than the affirmative plan. Counterplans are popular in American Policy and Parliamentary debate and are increasingly popular in Lincoln–Douglas Debate.

countervision (American Policy Debate)—a response to a Kritik argument's philosophical worldview or implication. For instance, a negative team might argue that the judge should endorse resistance to all forms of capitalism. An affirmative team might offer a countervision in which capitalism is modified in a way that minimizes exploitation of workers.

counterwarrant (American Policy Debate)—a reason to reject a debate resolution that is not necessarily a reason to reject the affirmative team's specific advocacy. For example, an affirmative team might support the resolution "Resolved: that the U.S. federal government should substantially increase space exploration" by advocating a manned mission to Mars. A negative team using a counterwarrant might respond that the resolution encompasses space exploration generally and that space exploration generally is bad. Alternatively, they might argue that other examples of the resolution (upgrading the space station or lunar mining) are disadvantageous, therefore, the resolution is not true. Affirmative teams often argue that counterwarrants are an illegitimate strategy, because time limits prevent thorough discussion of an entire resolution or of all of its possible examples.

coverage—the ability to successfully answer all opposing arguments in the allotted time. In some debate formats, students "cover" by speaking very quickly; in any format, word economy is necessary to make certain that no point goes unanswered.

criteria-goals case (American Policy Debate)—a style of affirmative case that begins with a consideration of the policy goals of the present system. The affirmative presents criteria that measure the fulfillment of those particular goals; the affirmative then shows that its proposed plan meets the criteria better than does the present system. For instance, on a medical care topic, an affirmative team might note that the acknowledged goals of the American health care system include universal coverage and efficient distribution of services, then argue that single-payer health care programs best meet those criteria.

critic-of-argument judging—a type of debate judge who prefers well-developed arguments and tends to disregard underdeveloped or unwarranted arguments, even if they are dropped by the opposing team. This contrasts with a blank slate approach, which accepts arguments as valid until they are refuted. Typically critic-of-argument judges regard themselves as educators rather than referees.

critique—*See* Kritik

cross-application—the use of an argument to answer multiple opposing arguments. For example, a negative team might argue that a plan to expand federal grant support for early-childhood education would exceed Congress's budget restrictions and that it would be an unacceptable increase in the power of the federal government. The affirmative could answer the first argument by noting that the plan is funded by private foundations; they could then cross-apply this response to the second argument.

cross-examination (American Policy Debate, Lincoln–Douglas Debate)—an interactive part of a policy or Lincoln–Douglas debate round in which debaters may ask their opponents questions. Cross-examination periods, which usually last 3 minutes, immediately follow an opponent's constructive speech. In policy debate:

- the second negative speaker questions the first affirmative speaker

- the first affirmative speaker questions the first negative speaker

- the first negative speaker questions the second affirmative speaker

- the second affirmative speaker questions the second negative speaker

Cross-examination questions attempt to clarify points ("Does your plan limit all campaign contributions or only contributions from corporations?"); to elicit further information ("Your second contention relies on the Marsden study. What was the sample size of that study?"); or to gain concessions that may be used to bolster an opposing argument ("If we prove that Russia will invade Ukraine with or without sanctions, don't we defeat your second advantage?").

Good cross-examinations avoid questions that invite a lengthy response ("Could you explain your plan?"); questions that are, in fact, poorly disguised arguments ("Isn't it true that most campaign finance reforms have failed?" "Are you aware that Saudi Arabia has called for the destruction of the State of Israel?"); or rhetorical questions ("How can you possibly argue that police forces never abuse their power?").

Cross-examination in Public Forum Debate is called "crossfire"; the speakers take turns posing questions to each other.

cross-examination (Mock Trial)—the questioning of a witness for one side of a case by the other side's attorney. Cross-examination attempts to expose flaws or contradictions in the witness's testimony or to elicit information not apparent from direct examination.

Cross Examination Debate Association (CEDA)—the larger of the two major American college policy debate organizations (the other being the National Debate Tournament), CEDA has several important functions. First,

CEDA sanctions more than 60 tournaments throughout the nation, including an annual National Championship Tournament (CEDA Nationals) that brings together more than 175 debate teams from across the nation to compete for a national championship. CEDA Nationals is regarded as the more inclusive and diverse of the two national tournaments. As it has no qualification procedures, entry is open to all. Second, CEDA takes the lead in formulating, in cooperation with the National Debate Tournament Committee, the annual intercollegiate policy debate topic used throughout the United States. Third, CEDA acts as a tournament-sanctioning agent, providing a framework for normalizing tournament practices and procedures. Additionally, throughout the tournament season, CEDA calculates the National Sweepstakes Standings, the national and regional rankings of member institutions based on compiled tournament results. Finally, CEDA serves as a professional association for scholars and teachers in the field of applied argumentation and debate. The organization sponsors scholarly programs at the annual convention of the National Communication Association and other professional meetings; it also publishes a refereed scholarly journal, *Contemporary Argumentation and Debate*, featuring monographs and essays addressing issues related to the theory and practice of academic debate.

CEDA was founded in 1971 as the Southwest Cross Examination Debate Association. For a number of years, CEDA debate was substantially different from NDT debate. For many years, CEDA employed a value debate format, as distinct from NDT's policy debate format; also, CEDA competition offered two topics each year, one for the fall semester and another for the spring. In 1995, CEDA and

NDT entered into a cooperative federation, effectively uniting American college policy debate; CEDA schools and NDT schools have since debated the same year-long policy topic and attended many of the same tournaments.

crossfire (Public Forum Debate)—the first two question-and-answer periods in Public Forum Debate. Crossfire differs from cross-examination in American Policy or Lincoln–Douglas debate in that both speakers may ask questions (and give answers). Generally, the first question is posed by the debater who has *not* just delivered a speech; beyond that, there is no prescribed order or alternation for questions, though the best crossfire periods will have close to an equal balance of questions and answers from both participants.

Crossfire questions attempt to clarify points ("Does your plan limit all campaign contributions, or only contributions from corporations?"); to elicit further information ("Your second contention relies on the Marsden study. What was the sample size of that study?"); or to gain concessions that may be used to bolster an opposing argument ("If we prove that Russia will invade Ukraine with or without sanctions, don't we defeat your second advantage?").

Good crossfire avoids questions that invite a lengthy response ("Could you explain your first contention?"); questions that are in fact poorly disguised arguments ("Isn't it true that most campaign finance reforms have failed?" "Are you aware that Saudi Arabia has called for the destruction of the State of Israel?"); or rhetorical questions ("How can you possibly argue that police forces never abuse their power?").

crystallization—distilling the arguments of a debate into a small number of critical issues. Crystallization occurs in the final speeches of all debate events, but is especially crucial in the second affirmative rebuttal in Lincoln–Douglas and the final focus speeches in Public Forum Debate.

CUSID—*See* Canadian University Society for Intercollegiate Debate

cutting evidence (American Policy Debate)—the production of policy debate evidence. The process consists of locating books or articles that might support particular arguments, identifying useful paragraphs or sentences from those sources, and transposing those excerpts into briefs. Originally, debaters photocopied source material and literally cut the appropriate paragraphs from the photocopies; later the "cut" evidence would be taped or pasted to paper or cards. *See also* evidence, piece of

D

data—statistics, observable facts, reasoning, or expert opinion that support a claim.

debatability standard—a means of judging whether an interpretation of the debate resolution is abusive; if a negative team cannot reasonably be expected to generate good counterarguments to a proposal, a judge might decide that the proposal is not topical. Examples of undebatable cases might include proposals so narrow that no counterevidence exists or proposals that are based on unpredictable interpretations of the resolution (a proposal on a health care resolution that supplies health care only to animals, for example).

debate—interactive argument intended to produce a conclusion or decision. All styles of formal competitive debate focus on a particular resolution or proposition, with one or more debaters speaking for that resolution, one or more opposing it, and one or more judges declaring a winner. Some styles of debate feature one resolution for the entire academic year, others prescribe a topic for one or two months, still others create a different topic for each debate. Speech times, judging criteria, and other rules also vary widely.

debate across the curriculum—the integration of debate practices—focused research, argument construction, public performance—into English, history, mathematics, and science classrooms. A history class might debate a resolution about the chief cause of the American Civil War; a science class might test the accuracy of a hypothesis regarding the spread of a disease. Many trends in education converge in this movement: the desire to highlight thinking/reasoning skills, rather than rote learning; the need to involve students in research-based projects; and the emphasis on performance as an expression of mastery of a subject. These pedagogical goals are congruent with a movement within the forensics community to expand beyond the narrow confines of elite tournament debating and teach the core skills of academic debate to a wider audience in both high schools and colleges.

Substantial academic literature supports the value of critical thinking and performance-based classroom tasks. Additionally, significant research supports the proposition that competing in debate events strengthens a student's overall academic performance. Studies have shown relationships between competition and cumulative grade point averages, graduation rates, and test scores; other observers have noted that debate competition improves the social skills of young students and strengthens their ability to withstand disappointments and setbacks.

debate camp—*See* debate workshop

debate institute—*See* debate workshop

debate workshop—an intensive training program for debaters generally held during the summer and hosted by a college or university debate program. Most workshops are for high school students, though some are directed at college debaters; they range in duration from a few days to (more commonly) two weeks or more. American Policy and Lincoln–Douglas debate workshops emphasize research on the coming year's topics; workshops in other formats teach basic speaking, research, and argument skills. International workshops teaching Worlds University Debate and Karl Popper Debate have become popular in recent years. Debate workshops are sometimes referred to as "debate institutes" or "debate camps."

decision calculus—a method of explaining how a debate judge might evaluate competing issues. If the affirmative argues that their proposal will reduce the risk of economic depression and improve national security, the negative might argue that the proposal would infringe on individual rights and could cause environmental harm. In subsequent speeches, particularly the last rebuttals, each team will try to prove a) that the other team's impacts will not occur, and b) that, even if they did occur, the impacts claimed on their own side of the flow are more compelling.

The criteria used to compare impacts include:

- *magnitude*: The affirmative team argues that their plan will save 3,000 lives each year. "We prove in our disadvantage argument that the environmental impact of the plan will cost at least 50,000 lives over the next ten years. That's a net loss of 20,000 lives."

- *probability*: "The evidence supporting the negative impact comes from a journalist from *TIME* magazine, who says the Ebola epidemic 'might spread' worldwide. Our evidence from distinguished epidemiologists says that the risk is 'very low.'"

- *time frame*: "The affirmative claims that their plan will create 100,000 jobs over the next five years. But they concede that the plan will also increase the risk of economic recession within the next year. So that will happen first, and it will destroy more jobs, and will make investors less likely to pump their capital into the affirmative plan."

- *reversibility*: "The negative claims that the affirmative plan will destroy jobs. Even if that is true, jobs can be regained. Life still goes on for unemployed persons. But the negative concedes that the affirmative proposal will save several thousand lives each year; those saved lives would otherwise have been lost and nothing brings those lives back."

decision rule (American Policy Debate)—a categorical instruction on how the judge should decide. "You must vote for the team that best increases individual rights" or "You must vote for the team that reduces unnecessary suffering" would be examples of decision rules.

declamation (Individual Events)—a competitive Individual Event in which a contestant presents a speech written by another. The speaker may choose a historic speech given by a famous public figure, a contemporary speech given at a commencement or memorial, or even a successful speech written for tournament competition. The speech is memorized and rehearsed. Declamation is rarely offered by college tournaments and is often used as a training event for middle school and younger high school competitors. In some leagues, declamation is known as "oratorical interpretation."

deduction—the process of reasoning from general statements or premises to reach a conclusion. In a deductive statement, if both initial statements and premises are true, then the conclusion must be true. (A classic example: "All men are mortal. James is a man. Therefore, James is mortal.") A chain of deductive reasoning is known as a syllogism. Deduction is distinct from induction, which infers general principles or probabilities from specific facts.

defendant (Mock Trial)—a person who is accused of violating a civil or criminal law. In Mock Trial, "defendant" refers to the team presenting the defense's case in court.

definitions—what the words of the debate resolution mean. Lincoln–Douglas and Public Forum debaters generally offer definitions proactively in the first affirmative speech. Usually these are drawn from general or specialized dictionaries or from experts who are discussing the topic. Negative teams may contest the affirmative definitions and provide their own.

delivery—the physical and vocal presentation of a speech. Physical delivery includes posture, relaxation or tension, and gestures. Vocal delivery includes projection, clarity of enunciation, and variations in pitch and pace.

deputy leader of the Opposition (DLO) (British Parliamentary Debate)—the second speaker for the Opposition. The deputy leader of the Opposition responds to arguments presented by the deputy prime minister.

deputy prime minister (DPM) (British Parliamentary Debate)—the second speaker for the Government. The deputy prime minister responds to arguments presented by the leader of the Opposition.

dilatory motion (Congressional Debate)—a motion whose purpose is to delay or avoid substantive debate; the presiding officer may rule such motions out of order.

dilemma—a forced choice of one of only two possible alternatives, either of which would be undesirable. For example: "If my opponent's plan succeeds in its attempt to strengthen Pakistan, it will enrage India, and increase the risk of war. If it fails to strengthen Pakistan, terrorist influence there will increase." Debaters sometimes refer to a dilemma as a "double bind."

dino (American Parliamentary Debate)—a former debater ("dinosaur") who returns to the debate activity to judge rounds.

direct examination (Mock Trial)—initial courtroom questioning of a witness for one side of a courtroom case by that side's attorney.

disadvantage (American Policy Debate)—an undesirable outcome of an affirmative plan. Disadvantage arguments are critical to many negative strategies. A disadvantage claims that, even if the affirmative proposal were to gain advantages, it would also have negative effects that would outweigh the positive effects. Disadvantages may address economic impacts ("New spending at this time would cause wide-ranging harm to the economy."); political impacts ("The plan would injure the president's credibility, making it impossible for him to achieve other, more important, policy goals."); or international impacts ("The trade agreement that the affirmative proposes may improve our relations with Japan, but it will injure our relations with China, and that relationship is more important.").

disclosure—providing advance information about one's affirmative case or negative positions. American Policy and Lincoln–Douglas debaters often post cases and positions on argument wikis (online collections of disclosed national circuit arguments). A few early-season tournaments require advance disclosure.

disclosure of decisions—a procedure in which the judge announces the decision at the conclusion of a debate in the presence of the debaters. Comments on the arguments themselves may or may not accompany disclosure. Some tournaments forbid disclosure of decisions and only publicize the record of wins and losses at the end of the tournament.

discourse—the words the debaters choose to present their arguments. Increasingly, debaters may criticize opponents' choice of language: a debaters' use of gendered language ("mankind" rather than "humankind" may be condemned as sexist, or the term "Oriental" may be criticized as demeaning to persons of Asian heritage).

discursive impact (American Policy Debate)—a claim that the effect of language used in the round should be evaluated before any of the policies advocated in the round. A debater might argue that debaters' language might reinforce various gendered or racist assumptions, that debaters should be role models in the use of language, and that judges should use their ballots to punish pejorative phrases and assumptions.

dispositionality (American Policy Debate)—a variant of conditionality in which the judge may "dispose" of, or exclude from his decision, a disadvantageous negative counterplan. Suppose that the affirmative team proposes increased federal funding for health care, and the negative team presents a dispositional counterplan saying that the states should increase funding instead. If the affirmative proves that state-level action is disadvantageous, the judge could simply disregard the counterplan and look to other issues (rather than considering the counterplan as a reason to vote against the negative team).

divide a motion (Congressional Debate)—to consider the parts of a bill separately. Division of a motion is not debatable and requires a majority vote.

division of labor (American Policy Debate)—a negative team's system of assigning the extension of specific arguments to specific speeches. For example, the second negative speaker might discuss solvency and a disadvantage, while the first negative rebuttalist discusses topicality and the counterplan.

division of the house (Congressional Debate)—a call for an actual show of hands, rather than a voice vote. A member who believes that the outcome of a voice vote is uncertain might call for a division of the house.

DLO—*See* deputy leader of the Opposition

docket (Congressional Debate)—a collection of bills and resolutions to be debated. Generally, a docket of legislation is presented to participating teams several weeks in advance of competition to allow debaters to research and strategize. A committee of coaches may modify or eliminate some items from the docket altogether before a final agenda is presented to the chamber.

double bind—*See* dilemma

double entry—a student who enters more than one event at a given tournament; typically, one debate event and one speech event or multiple individual speech events.

double octafinal round—an elimination round consisting of 32 teams; the 16 winners would proceed to the octafinal round.

double turnaround (American Policy Debate)—when an affirmative team contradicts both the link and impact premises of a negative argument, inadvertently creating a new disadvantage to their own position. For example, the negative team might argue that the affirmative proposal would increase overall government spending and that increased spending is bad. A double turnaround would occur if the affirmative were to argue that a) their proposal decreases overall government spending, and then argue that b) increased spending is good. A negative team could then grant both affirmative responses and note that the affirmative has just argued that their own proposal is disadvantageous, because it reduces desirable spending.

DPM—*See* deputy prime minister

dramatic interpretation (Individual Events)—a high school interpretive event in which students present a dramatic excerpt from a published novel, story, play, or screenplay, delivered from memory. Dramatic interpretation pieces usually feature multiple characters with different voices. No manuscripts, props, or costumes may be used, and a 10-minute time limit is imposed. Precise diction, vocal range, expressive physical delivery, intelligent character development, and thoughtful pacing are all key characteristics of a successful dramatic interp.

drop—to lose to, to be voted down. ("We dropped to Texas Tech last round." "The judge dropped us.") Or, to fail to answer an argument ("My opponents have dropped the first disadvantage that my partner argued.").

dropped argument—an argument left unanswered by the opposing team. Most judges treat dropped arguments as conceded arguments, so they may be crucial in determining the winner of a debate.

duo interpretation (Individual Events)—a speech event in which a pair of performers interpret a short piece of dramatic literature. A duo may be either serious, humorous, or some combination of the two. Performers may interact only vocally; no eye contact or physical contact is permitted. Props and costumes are not permitted. Each participant may vocalize multiple characters. Dramatic duo pieces consist of excerpts of published television, screen, or stage plays, heavily edited to highlight dramatic interaction and fit within the event's 10-minute maximum time limit.

education standard (American Policy Debate)—a topicality argument that says that a debate resolution should be interpreted in a way most likely to increase the education of the debaters. A negative team eager to protect itself against unusual cases might argue that the resolution should be strictly interpreted—that a narrow range of cases allows for deeper research and discussion and that depth and predictability make the activity more educational. An affirmative team might respond by saying that a broad topic exposes debaters to more ideas and increases critical thinking skills.

elections disadvantage (American Policy Debate)—a type of politics disadvantage, frequently argued in election years. An elections disadvantage argues that the passage of the affirmative plan would increase or decrease the popularity of a political party or its candidates, thereby creating an undesirable shift in political power. For instance, the affirmative might propose a program of immigration reform. The negative might argue that such a program would be deeply unpopular in border states and would cause voters in those states to elect extremely conservative candidates to Congress. The negative would then argue that a more conservative Congress would enact harmful legislation or block necessary legislation. In a presidential election year, an elections disadvantage might argue that such a backlash would cause one candidate to prevail over another, with adverse results.

Affirmative responses to election disadvantages would include challenges to the argument's uniqueness—for example, conservatives will be elected to office with or without the plan or the harmful legislation under discussion will be passed regardless. The affirmative might also argue that the perception created by the affirmative plan will be negligible or that it will be the opposite of what the negative assumes. Finally, the affirmative may argue that the legislative result of the election will be good, not bad—that the legislation the negative alleges to be harmful is, in fact, beneficial.

elimination round—*See* elimination round bracket

elimination round bracket—"sudden death" debates, in which the winner advances to a subsequent round, while the loser leaves the competition. Brackets may consist of the top 4, 8, 16, or 32 teams (depending on the size of the tournament) and are constructed in a "power protection" format; in the first elimination round, the top-ranked team debates the lowest-ranked elimination round team, the second-ranked team debates the second-lowest-ranked team, and so on. Elimination rounds are heard by panels of judges (usually three or five) and often draw spectators.

Emory switch (American Policy Debate)—a reversal of the traditional negative division of labor: the first negative constructive presents disadvantages to the affirmative plan, while the second negative constructive makes arguments against harm, inherency, and solvency.

empirically denied—the claim that an advantage or disadvantage has not occurred in the past, therefore, it will not occur in the future. The negative team might argue that economic decline increases the risk of war; the affirmative might respond that previous declines have not led to war, therefore, the disadvantage is empirically denied.

enabling planks (American Policy Debate)—sections of an affirmative plan that describe how funding, enforcement, and other necessary conditions for plan action will be carried out.

enforcement plank (American Policy Debate)—a part of the affirmative plan providing assurance that the plan's mandates will be carried out, usually through a directive that a particular agency will oversee and ensure compliance with those mandates. A plank may include specific penalties or may simply state that enforcement will occur through "normal means."

English Speaking Union (ESU)—an international educational charity founded in Britain in 1918. The ESU promotes a variety of activities, including debating, public speaking, and student exchange programs; runs conferences and seminars; and offers scholarships to encourage the effective use of the English language around the globe. The ESU is best-known for its major educational activity: the promotion of debate as an educational tool. The English-Speaking Union Centre for Speech and Debate, established in 1995 to coordinate the organization's work in persuasive spoken English, is one of the world's major supporters of formal debate. In the United Kingdom, it runs the national championships in debating for schools (the ESU Schools Mace, the largest and oldest competition of its kind in the world) and universities (the John Smith Memorial Mace, named after a former Labour Party leader who was a member of the 1962 championship team). The ESU also provides teacher training and support to overseas

English Speaking Unions and selects and trains the England Schools Debating Team, which competes in the World Schools Debating Championships each year.

enthymeme—a syllogism that omits or implies one of its premises rather than stating that premise directly. An enthymeme is logically incomplete because the speaker believes that the audience will assume the truth of the missing claim. For example, a speaker might claim that a politician who opposes government-sponsored health care must be a conservative; the unexpressed premise, which the speaker assumes that the audience believes, is that only conservatives oppose government-sponsored health care. Time constraints in forensics usually dictate the use of enthymemes rather than full expression of all an argument's premises; of course, advocates must choose carefully in deciding which premises might be omitted.

equity officer (Parliamentary Debate)—a tournament official charged with assuring fair treatment for all participants—often with particular attention to race and gender issues.

ESU—*See* English Speaking Union

ethos—one of Aristotle's basic rhetorical categories; ethos refers to the credibility or trustworthiness of the speaker. Ethos can be divided into initial ethos and derived ethos. In competitive forensics, initial ethos might include the speaker's appearance (grooming and appropriate dress); the projection of friendliness and self-confidence; or association with a successful team or school. Speakers then proceed to derive ethos by speaking with clarity and fluency, using appropriate language, and displaying familiarity with the topic and a command of relevant facts.

EUDC—*See* European Universities Debating Championship

European Square Debate (Parliamentary Debate)—a type of Parliamentary Debate that simulates actual public policy discussion between major European nations. Four teams, each representing a major European country, debate a policy resolution. Two teams (for instance, France and the United Kingdom) form a coalition in favor of the resolution, with the other two teams (for instance, Denmark and Russia) aligned in opposition. Each team will advance its own arguments for or against the resolution, while respecting and attempting to advance the arguments made by its coalition partner.

Each team is composed of two speakers—the Prime Minister and the Foreign Secretary. Which team in the coalition speaks first is determined at random. In this example, the debate may start with the Prime Minister of France (the affirmative side), followed by the Prime Minister of Denmark (the opposition side), followed by the second speaker of France and the second speaker of Denmark. The debate continues with the first speaker of the United Kingdom, followed by the first speaker of Russia and the respective second speakers. Each debater speaks for 5 minutes. Points of information may be presented to any speaker by any opposing speaker.

European Universities Debating Championship (EUDC) (British Parliamentary Debate)—an annual debate competition. Although most teams in attendance are from European universities, in recent years the tournament has included some teams from the Middle East and Central Asia. The competition, which uses the British Parliamentary Debate format, is held in late summer each year. At the first tournament, held in 1999, only 30 teams attended;

in 2013, more than 200 teams attended. EUDC is governed by a council of the competing students (one per nation); this council facilitates communication between member debate clubs and runs the annual championship tournament.

evaluative argument—an attempt to persuade an audience that something is good or bad, usually based on particular criteria, which might include ethical, practical, and aesthetic considerations.

even if—a phrase commonly heard in late rebuttal speeches, when a speaker is attempting to provide several independent reasons why the judge should vote for her arguments. ("Even if you don't believe that our plan reduces tensions in the South China Sea, consider the trade arguments, which we're winning handily." "We think the affirmative plan causes a short-term risk of regional war. Even if you don't agree, consider the other side of the flow, where we prove that the plan will worsen our trade deficit, not improve it.")

evidence—data that form the basis for conclusions. Evidence may include personal observation, current and historical examples, statistics, and expert opinion. Evidence used in competitive speech and debate usually consists of statistics and statements from experts quoted or paraphrased from published sources.

evidence, piece of (American Policy Debate)—the card, cite, and tag used in support of an argument in policy debate. A piece of evidence includes a quotation from a reliable source (the card), a citation that includes all of the information an opponent or judge needs to find the evidence and to evaluate the source (the cite), and a concise statement that summarizes the thesis of the quotation and states its significance in the debate (the tag).

example of the resolution (American Policy Debate)—a specific instance or model of resolutional action. Typically, policy debaters defend one example of the debate resolution in any particular debate round rather than attempting to prove the truth of a general statement. For instance, on a policy resolution that states that the U.S. federal government should increase investment in transportation infrastructure, the affirmative might argue for the repair of roads and bridges, the expansion of ports, or the construction of high-speed rail systems.

exclusion counterplan (American Policy Debate)—negative advocacy that generally supports the affirmative proposal but excludes certain populations, regions, or actions. For instance, the affirmative might support a resolution that calls on the government to provide employment for all citizens; a negative counterplan might provide employment but exclude tax evaders or drug addicts.

exhibit (Mock Trial)—a document, record, or other physical object formally introduced as evidence. Exhibits are included in the case packet presented to both teams several weeks in advance of the tournament.

existential inherency (American Policy Debate)—an inherency argument that observes that a significant harm has continued in the status quo for an extended period but specifies neither a structure keeping the harm in place nor attitudes that ensure its resilience. Existential inherency argues that, while we may not know precisely why the harm continues, we know that it does continue—that is enough warrant for a significant change.

expository speaking (Individual Events)—a competitive Individual Event in which speakers present prepared speeches meant to inform the audience. Expository topics are wide-ranging and may include a new invention or trend, a historical event or figure, a scientific process, or a concept. The speaker's goal is to simplify a complex topic or to approach a familiar topic in a new and revealing way. Many leagues permit expository speakers to use visual aids in their presentations. Expository speeches are memorized and rehearsed and are 8–10 minutes in length. Expository speaking is often referred to as "informative speaking."

extemp—*See* extemporaneous speaking

extemporaneous commentary (Individual Events)—a competitive Individual Event in which contestants are given a current events topic; they then prepare a speech that presents an opinion or perspective on that topic. Typically, speakers have 15 minutes to prepare a 5-minute speech. Extemporaneous commentary differs from extemporaneous speaking in that the topic is not phrased as a question, so speakers have more freedom to comment on the topic as they choose. Extemporaneous commentary is inspired by the work of television media commentators; the speech is usually presented sitting down.

extemporaneous debate (Individual Events)—a supplementary event offered at the National Speech and Debate Association national tournament. Extemporaneous debate resembles a much-abbreviated one-on-one form of American Parliamentary Debate. The topics are announced only 30 minutes before competition begins. Entry is limited to students who have been eliminated from competition in another speech or debate event. Debaters may conduct research prior to the debate and may quote evidence verbatim.

In extemporaneous debate, the proposition (or affirmative) debater must uphold the resolution. The opposition (or negative) debater must oppose the resolution and/or the proposition debater's case.

The debate proceeds as follows:

Proposition Constructive	2 minutes
Cross-Examination of Proposition	1 minute
Opposition Constructive	2 minutes
Cross-Examination of Opposition	1 minute
Mandatory Prep Time	1 minute
Proposition Rebuttal	2 minutes
Opposition Rebuttal	2 minutes
Mandatory Prep Time	1 minute
Proposition Rebuttal	2 minutes
Opposition Rebuttal	2 minutes

extemporaneous speaking (extemp) (Individual Events)— a competitive Individual Event in which contestants have limited preparation time (usually 30 minutes) to produce a speech on a current events topic. Typically, speakers have a choice of three current events topics, each phrased as a question ("How will recent budget reductions affect the stock market?"; "Does the reelection of Benjamin Netanyahu doom any Middle East peace plan?"). They then have 30 minutes to prepare a 7-minute speech, using any source materials they have brought to the contest; they are ranked in comparison with four to six other speakers. Contestants with the best ranks after several preliminary rounds of competition then advance to one or more elimination rounds. Many tournaments follow the National Speech and Debate Association's (NSDA, formerly the NFL) practice of dividing extemporaneous speaking into International Extemp (foreign affairs topics) and United States Extemp (topics dealing with U.S. political and economic issues). Strong extemporaneous speeches demonstrate good organization, verbal fluency, and deep knowledge of the topic.

extension—further development of an argument made in a previous speech. ("Please extend my partner's third argument, to which my opponents have not responded; this proves that the federal government is already increasing funding for early-childhood education, so my opponents' plan is not necessary.")

extratopicality (American Policy Debate)—a proposal that meets the terms of the resolution but then includes additional action beyond its purview. For example, if the resolution requires the United States to reduce military assistance to Middle Eastern nations, a plan that also reduced economic assistance would be extratopical, as would a plan that also reduced military assistance to countries in East Asia or sub-Saharan Africa. Extratopical action is generally regarded as illegitimate. A negative team might argue that the affirmative team should lose the debate, because they have gone beyond the resolution, or they might argue that the judge should ignore the extratopical action and any advantages that might result from it.

F

fairness standard (American Policy Debate)—an argument maintaining that a debate resolution should be interpreted in a way that ensures that each side has a reasonable chance to win the round. For instance, if the resolution is "The U.S. federal government should provide health care assistance to U.S. citizens," the negative might claim that the government must assist not merely some but *all* citizens, including those who have no need of assistance; the affirmative might answer that this would place an unfair burden on the affirmative.

fallacy—a logical error. Common fallacies include: ad hominem, argument from authority, begging the question, circular reasoning, naturalistic fallacy, and post hoc ergo propter hoc. *See* individual fallacies

fiat power (American Policy Debate)—an assumed power to put a proposal into effect; a legal mandate binding on the parties involved, overriding their personal attitudes. The concept of debate fiat stems from the word "should" in a policy resolution; it is the desirability of the proposal that is under discussion, not whether the proposal would actually be adopted. For example, the current U.S. Congress would never approve the legalization of marijuana; debaters, however, concern themselves not with whether that would happen, but whether it should happen. Debaters often declare that their proposals are to be implemented "by fiat" as a means of directing the debate to "should" questions rather than "would" questions. Fiat power is limited to the scope of the resolution and to matters subject to government power; it is not a "magic wand" to avoid substantive argument. For instance, an affirmative team may fiat that the U.S. government will expand health care assistance to developing nations; they cannot fiat that sufficient doctors and nurses will agree to be hired, that diseases will be cured, or that foreign governments that oppose such assistance will suddenly accept it.

field context definition (American Policy Debate)—an interpretation of a word or phrase in the resolution that is derived from the writings of experts on the topic. For instance, debaters may wish to argue that a resolution using the term "economic assistance" should not include emergency humanitarian aid. No dictionary definition is likely to address this distinction, but an article in which an expert explains the difference would provide good support.

file—a collection of prepared arguments on a specific subtopic ("Could you hand me the Kurdistan file?" "We need to update our voting rights file.").

final focus (Public Forum Debate)—the last speech given by each team in a Public Forum round (originally known as "the last shot"). The final focus speech is 2 minutes long. Typically, this speech attempts to isolate one or two reasons why a team is winning the round and makes crucial comparisons between the two teams' arguments and evidence.

final round—the last round of a tournament, featuring only the two top-performing teams (or, in Individual Events, the six or seven top contestants) and usually judged by several specially chosen judges. Some tournaments invite persons with special expertise on the topic to judge final rounds. At most tournaments, this is one of the few rounds that might actually attract a large audience.

first affirmative constructive (American Policy Debate)—the first speech in a policy debate. This speech presents the affirmative plan and outlines its advantages, taking care to satisfy all the stock issues. Typically, the first affirmative constructive is the only completely prepared speech in the round.

first affirmative rebuttal (American Policy Debate)— the sixth speech, and second rebuttal, in a policy debate. The first affirmative rebuttal is considered to be one of the most challenging speeches in policy debate because it follows two consecutive negative speeches and must answer all of the arguments presented in those speeches.

first affirmative speaker (American Policy Debate)—the speaker who begins a policy debate, presenting the plan and advantages; this speaker also presents the first affirmative rebuttal.

first negative constructive (American Policy Debate)— the second speech in a policy debate. This speech introduces the complete range of arguments in the negative strategy, which may include arguments against the affirmative advantages, topicality arguments, disadvantages, counterplans, and Kritiks.

first negative rebuttal (American Policy Debate)—the fifth speech in a policy debate. The first negative rebuttal extends selected arguments that were introduced in the first negative constructive (other arguments are extended by the preceding speech, the second negative constructive).

first negative speaker (American Policy Debate)—the second speaker in a policy debate round. This speaker offers the opening arguments against the affirmative case and also presents the first negative rebuttal.

flashing—sharing written materials with a partner, opponent, or judge in the round by means of a flash drive. The practice is increasingly common in American Policy and Lincoln–Douglas debate. Time spent flashing may or may not be counted against a debater's preparation time.

flex case (Public Forum Debate)—a strategic approach in Public Forum Debate in which the second-speaking team directly refutes their opponent's case instead of presenting their own. Flex casing requires researching and drafting a wide range of prepared blocks on both sides of the resolution, then choosing, in-round, the blocks that most effectively counter an opponent's case.

flex prep—*See* flex preparation

flex preparation (Lincoln–Douglas Debate)—a variation on preparation time, most often used in Lincoln–Douglas Debate, in which cross-examination and preparation time are merged and may be used for either purpose. For example, a speaker might choose to use only 1 minute for cross-examination and apply the other 2 minutes to his preparation time. Conversely, the speaker might forfeit some of his preparation time and extend the cross-examination. Sometimes called "flex prep."

flighting—scheduling two consecutive contests in the same room with the same judge or judges. This happens most commonly in American high school tournaments that offer a variety of different debate formats. Policy debate rounds take between 90 minutes and 2 hours to complete, but Lincoln–Douglas and Public Forum rounds take approximately half that time; so these events are frequently flighted. This practice reduces the number of rooms and judges that are necessary to conduct any given round. Pairings specify that certain rounds will happen during the "A" flight, with a "B" flight held immediately after the "A" flight round is concluded.

flip—to turn or reverse an opponent's impact. ("They argue that their plan will increase economic growth. We flip that impact; economic growth is bad, because it increases fossil fuel emissions which endanger the planet.")

flip—a coin toss that decides which side each team will represent in a round. In most debate formats, flips are reserved for elimination rounds (unless the two teams have debated previously, in which case they reverse sides from their previous meeting). National Forensic League rules for Public Forum mandate that a coin flip be used before all rounds. The winner of the flip may choose the side that her team will represent. In Public Forum, the winner of the flip may choose to speak first or second, leaving the decision regarding the side to the opponent.

flip round—a debate round in which the sides (affirmative or negative, pro or con, Government or Opposition) are decided by the contestants' flipping a coin.

floor (Congressional Debate)—the part of a legislative chamber from which members speak; also, the right to speak. A Congressional debater who has been recognized by the chair is said to "have the floor."

floor vote (Parliamentary Debate)—a decision rendered by members of the audience; sometimes used in final rounds at Parliamentary tournaments; also known as a "rising vote."

flowing—a system of note-taking used during a debate round. Generally, individual speeches are flowed in vertical columns, with responses to opposing arguments flowed horizontally next to the arguments they answer. Traditional Lincoln–Douglas and Public Forum flows usually require one or two pieces of paper; some Lincoln–Douglas and Parliamentary and most policy debaters and judges might use 8–10 pages per round (with one page each for different parts of the affirmative case, and a page for each negative disadvantage, counterplan, topicality argument, or Kritik argument).

Here is one page of the first three speeches of a policy debate flow. Evidence cited is referred to by an author's name and year.

1AC	1NC	2AC

OB 1
INHERENCY

Currently lack of ——→ 1. Old evidence ———→ Even more true now with
public investment budget sequester
precludes road and
bridge repair 2. Evidence concerns ——→ 1. No evidence of
Barron's 11-3-09 only federal significant state action
government—states 2. States are broke
are acting Reich 2012

PLAN: US fed govt
should increase
transportation spending
by $50 billion over the
next five years

ADVANTAGE I: BRIDGE
AND ROAD REPAIR
BOOSTS THE ECONOMY

The construction ——→ 1. Their evidence is ——→ Their evidence is quoting
industry is in a slump old; recovery now Obama administration
Barrons 4-13-13 NYT 7-21-13 propaganda

2. New housing starts ——→ 1. Propaganda, as above
= recovery 2. Congress is slashing
WASH POST 7-28-23 spending, putting brakes
on recovery
Reich 2012

New construction ——→ 1. The jobs will be ——→ Jobs will be 3–5 years;
jobs will jump-start temporary; little real that is plenty
consumer spending advantage
Rivlin 2010 2. Massive govt ———→ 1. No risk of inflation
programs risk inflation currently
Cato Institute 2009 Summers 6-20-13
2. Govt can easily resist
inflation
Feldstein 2009
Harms of unemployment
far worse than harms of
inflation
Garrett 2012

flow judge—an experienced debate judge, generally a coach or former debater, who takes extensive notes during the debate, often including the details of complex arguments and evidence citations. Flow judges are distinct from lay or community judges, who generally do not take extensive notes and emphasize speaking and rhetoric over detailed argument.

forensics—the usual generic term for competitive speech and debate competition, derived from the Latin *forensic*, meaning "of the forum"; the broader English definition of the adjective "forensic" means "of public debate or argument." The term is occasionally used to refer just to speech events as distinct from debate events.

framework—an argument that describes what the judge should decide, and how the judge should decide it. Some policy debate framework arguments claim that a judge should decide between competing policies and should reject purely philosophical arguments. In Lincoln–Douglas, a debater might argue that the judge should evaluate the resolution as a general statement or that the debate should center on ethical issues rather than practical applications.

friendly question (Congressional Debate)—a question directed to a Congressional debater who shares the questioner's position. Such a question effectively grants the respondent more time to expand on her argument.

frontline (American Policy Debate)—a group of initial affirmative responses to a particular negative argument—generally presented in the second affirmative constructive.

functional competition (American Policy Debate)—functional competition occurs when a counterplan's essential action provides a reason why the affirmative plan should be rejected. Functional competition contrasts with textual competition, which requires that the text of a counterplan contradict the text of the affirmative plan. A consult counterplan, for example, would be functionally competitive (it approaches the problem with a different solution, e.g., consulting other nations before acting) but would not be textually competitive (since no affirmative plan explicitly refuses to consult before acting). Generally, a negative team will prefer functional competition as a standard, while an affirmative team will prefer textual competition.

future abuse (American Policy Debate)—a topicality argument that asserts that although the affirmative's interpretation of the resolution may not create unfairness in the current debate round, it might lead to unfair practices in some future round. Generally, the negative argues that a liberal interpretation of a word or phrase in the resolution might lead to impermissibly liberal interpretations in future rounds, therefore, the judge should not accept the present interpretation.

G

games theory (American Policy Debate)—a philosophy of judging that grants special emphasis to procedural issues, particularly issues of fairness. A games theory judge is likely to regard questions of competitive equity and reciprocal burdens and be especially likely to vote against teams who have illegitimately expanded affirmative or negative ground.

garden path (British Parliamentary Debate)—a series of questions designed to lead an opponent to a specific, damaging, admission.

gavel (Congressional Debate)—a small mallet used by a judge or presiding officer to open or close a session; "to gavel" is to request or maintain order. In Congressional Debate, a gavel may also be used to communicate time signals to a speaker—one tap of the gavel indicating that 1 minute remains; two taps indicating that 30 seconds remain.

general knowledge standard (British Parliamentary Debate, Parliamentary Debate)—a way of judging the acceptability of a case or counterplan. A case is debatable if a knowledgeable, well-informed college graduate would be able to generate reasonable arguments against that case. Cases that require opponents to possess esoteric or technical knowledge are arguably undebatable.

generic argument (American Policy Debate)—a negative argument, usually a disadvantage or Kritik, that can be applied to a wide range of affirmative cases. For instance, a generic economic disadvantage can be argued against any affirmative proposal that increases federal spending; a generic Kritik of imperialism can be argued against any affirmative proposal that increases American military power.

geography (Congressional Debate)—a method of deciding which Congressional debater should speak next. A presiding officer using the geographic method will be sure to call on speakers from different locations in the chamber, keeping in mind that speakers for and against the legislation should alternate.

Government (British Parliamentary Debate, Parliamentary Debate)—the affirmative team in a Parliamentary Debate. The Government team begins the debate with a case that supports the resolution. Sometimes referred to as "the proposition."

Government whip (British Parliamentary Debate)—the last speaker for the Government. The whip summarizes the Government's case and answers the key Opposition objections.

grace period (Individual Events, Parliamentary Debate)—the additional 30 seconds that a speaker may use without being penalized.

grand crossfire (Public Forum Debate)—the final cross-examination period. Grand crossfire takes place after the two summary speeches, but before the two final focus speeches. The debaters are generally seated rather than standing, and all four participants may ask and answer questions. The give-and-take of grand crossfire is quite informal; interruptions are permitted, though the speakers attempt to strike a balance between lively energy and order.

ground standard (American Policy Debate)—a topicality argument that asserts that an affirmative interpretation of the resolution must not deprive the negative team of adequate ground for opposing arguments. The negative might argue that an affirmative plan that made only very small changes in the status quo would evade most counterarguments, thus making actual debate difficult.

group discussion (Individual Events)—an event offered at a number of local and state tournaments. General topic areas are announced prior to the tournament, and students prepare by reading about these; specific questions for discussion, however, are not announced until the beginning of each round. A general topic area might be education reform; a question for a particular round might be, "What are the best methods for improving the quality of teaching?" Contestants may bring notes and articles into the competition. After the topic is revealed, students are given 5 minutes to formulate their argument and draw for speaking order; speakers then have a limited amount of time (typically 2 minutes) to deliver an opening statement. A general discussion period (30–45 minutes) follows in which speakers attempt to work cooperatively to arrive at a useful answer to the question posed. A group consists of 5–7 contestants; judges rank the contestants first through last based on topic knowledge and an ability to formulate arguments and also on a contestant's ability to work toward a common goal.

grouping—a method of refutation that bundles similar arguments and answers them together. ("Group all of the arguments that my opponent makes against our disadvantage. I have two responses.")

H

harm (American Policy Debate)—one of the standard points of controversy, or stock issues, in policy debate. The term "harm" refers to an undesirable condition that an affirmative team attempts to solve. A harm might consist of cost or injury borne by individuals or by society as a whole. For example, an affirmative team defending the expansion of health care might address unnecessary death, low-quality care, and high emergency room costs as harms in the present system. The negative team would attempt to deny or minimize the existence of these harms.

hasty generalization—arriving at a general conclusion from a faulty examination of data or examples. A debater may argue that her opponent has chosen only a biased set of examples, too few examples, or unrepresentative examples. ("My opponent argues that most Roman Catholics ignore church teachings; in fact, he is only discussing American Roman Catholics, not Catholics from all over the world.") In policy or Lincoln–Douglas debate, the term is used as a criticism of the use of examples of the resolution ("The affirmative team assumes that the construction of lunar colonies is a typical example of space development; you can't prove the truth of the resolution by focusing on one unusual example.").

heckling (British Parliamentary Debate)—brief, clever, critical interruptions of an opponent's speech; permitted and even encouraged in British Parliamentary Debate.

highlighting—condensing or editing quoted material presented in a round. Highlighting is generally accepted if it does not omit significant context and if the author's conclusions are accurately represented.

high-low speaker points—the speaker point total accrued by a team after its high and low performances have been factored out. For instance, a team that is awarded 330 total speaker points over six rounds would have 220 high-low points after its high (58 points in one round) and its low (52 points in another round) are subtracted. Most tournaments prefer high-low points to total points as a means of determining awards and seeding.

hit—to be paired against in a contest; "We're hitting Central Catholic next round."

humorous interpretation (Individual Events)—a high school interpretive event in which students present a humorous excerpt from a novel, story, or play delivered from memory. Humorous interpretation pieces usually feature multiple characters with different voices. No manuscripts, props, or costumes may be used, and there is a 10-minute time limit. Precise diction, vocal range, expressive physical delivery, and thoughtful pacing are all key characteristics of a successful humorous interpretation.

hung case (Parliamentary Debate)—presenting only part of the Government's case in the first speech and completing it in the second. Hung cases are generally considered illegitimate; some leagues ban them.

hypothesis testing (American Policy Debate)—a theory that compares debate resolutions to scientific hypotheses. This analogy has several implications. First, a debate resolution, like a scientific hypothesis, is considered false until proven true; second, a resolution, again like a hypothesis, receives its most arduous testing through comparison to competing hypotheses (or counterplans). Finally, since competing hypotheses might contradict each other, a negative team need not provide a consistent position—they need only provide reasons why the resolution might not be true.

IDEA—*See* International Debate Education Association

impact—an identifiable result of a policy, belief, or value; the reason why an action or belief is good or bad. Impacts might include war, disease, economic depression, environmental destruction, violations of human rights, and dehumanization. Affirmative teams will argue for policies, values, or ideas that seek to prevent these impacts; negative teams will argue that the affirmative position will fail to solve for them or will cause larger negative impacts.

impact calculus—a method of explaining how a debate judge might evaluate competing issues. If the affirmative argues that their proposal will reduce the risk of economic depression and improve national security, the negative might argue that the proposal would infringe on individual rights and cause environmental harm. In subsequent speeches, particularly the last rebuttals, each team will try to prove a) that the other team's impacts will not occur and b) that, even if they did occur, the impacts claimed on their own side of the flow are more compelling. The criteria used to compare impacts include magnitude, probability, reversibility, and time frame. Impact calculus is sometimes known as "decision calculus." *See also* magnitude, reversibility, time frame

impact turnaround (American Policy Debate)—a reversal of an opponent's impact. A negative disadvantage might claim that the affirmative plan causes an economic downturn, with resultant loss of employment and income. The affirmative team might present a turnaround to this impact, claiming that an economic downturn will reduce the burning of fossil fuels and lessen environmental destruction. Impact turnarounds attempt to transform disadvantages into additional advantages for an affirmative team. They may also be applied to links to counterplans or Kritiks.

implementation specification (I-spec) (American Policy Debate)—a negative argument that accuses the affirmative of inadequately explaining the details of plan implementation and claims that the affirmative should lose the round because it is impossible for a judge to determine whether it would solve for the harm, or impossible for the negative to make specific arguments regarding solvency.

impromptu speaking (Individual Events)—a competitive Individual Event that emphasizes quick thinking and spontaneity. Contestants in impromptu are presented with a topic and then have 1–3 minutes to prepare a 4–6 minute speech that presents an organized, well-spoken response to that topic. Topics may be words, phrases, declarative sentences, questions, or objects. The method of developing the topic is up to the contestant, but the speech should be fluent and well-organized; it must interpret the topic in some creative way without drifting too far from it.

indicts—criticisms of an author or publication used as evidence. Indicts may include questioning an author's qualifications in the field, noting the prevalent bias of an author or publication, or criticizing the methodology or assumptions of an academic study.

Individual Events—the range of competitive speaking events as opposed to debate events. Individual Events fall into three categories:

- limited preparation events, in which a contestant is presented with a topic and must quickly prepare a speech on that topic. Limited preparation events test students' ability to think and organize under pressure and to speak clearly and eloquently without notes or manuscript. Extemporaneous and impromptu speaking are the two major limited preparation events, but several other events are often offered in certain regions or as supplemental or novelty events at national tournaments. These include: extemporaneous commentary, extemporaneous debate, and group discussion.

- platform events, in which students present speeches they have written and memorized. Platform events include original oratory, expository speaking, and rhetorical criticism.

- interpretive events, in which contestants read or perform from memory brief excerpts of literary prose, poetry, and/or drama. Interpretive events include duo interpretation, humorous interpretation, dramatic interpretation, poetry interpretation, prose interpretation, program oral interpretation, and extemporaneous interpretation.

See Appendix; *See also* the specific events

induction—a type of reasoning that constructs or infers general principles or probabilities from specific facts and examples. For instance, if I examine 20 state governments that have increased the length of prison sentences, and then observe that in 16 of these states crime has decreased,

I might reasonably conclude that longer prison sentences deter crime. Inductive reasoning contrasts with deductive reasoning, in which specific examples are derived from general propositions.

informative speaking (Individual Events)—a competitive Individual Event in which speakers present prepared speeches meant to inform the audience. Informative topics are wide-ranging and may include a new invention or trend, a historical event or figure, a scientific process, or a concept. The speaker's goal is to simplify a complex topic or to approach a familiar topic in a new and revealing way. Some leagues permit informative speakers to use visual aids in their presentations. Informative speeches are memorized and rehearsed, and are 8–10 minutes in length. Informative speaking is often referred to as "expository speaking."

inherency (American Policy Debate)—the state of being an intrinsic, necessary part of a system. Inherency is one of the standard points of controversy, or stock issues, in a policy debate—where the term is used to describe a feature of the status quo that exists and will continue to exist in the absence of the affirmative plan. Inherency can be either structural or attitudinal. Structural inherency means that a legal structure (or absence of one) prevents the status quo from solving for the harm. As an example, consider a case that addresses the quality of life for gay and lesbian citizens. For many years, gays and lesbians could not receive their partners' U.S. government benefits; the Defense of Marriage Act was the legal structure that kept that harm in place. Attitudinal inherency means that an attitude—held by lawmakers or the general public—causes the harm to continue. The fact that many people dislike gays and lesbians and tend to discriminate or speak out against them would be an example of attitudinal inherency. An affirmative team would argue that, in the present system, these inherent conditions will perpetuate the harm (but that the plan can solve for those conditions). A negative team might respond that no genuine legal or attitudinal barrier exists now—or, alternatively, that the plan cannot solve for the effect of the inherent conditions the affirmative describes.

in-round abuse (American Policy Debate)—a topicality argument that asserts that the affirmative's interpretation of the resolution creates significant abuse in the debate round. The negative might argue, for instance, that the affirmative approach is so unpredictable that the negative could not reasonably anticipate it and prepare to debate it, or they might argue that the affirmative case has been designed to leave little room for debate.

intellectual endorsement (American Policy Debate)—a framework argument that asks the judge to cast her ballot for or against a philosophical position rather than for or against a policy proposal (such as the affirmative plan). Intellectual endorsement arguments are usually presented by Kritik debaters. For example, a debater might argue that the affirmative plan is grounded in capitalism and that the judge should vote negative to endorse the view that capitalism is philosophically unacceptable.

International Debate Education Association (IDEA)— a global network of organizations that promote debate as a social and educational tool. IDEA believes that debate promotes mutual understanding and informed citizenship around the world and that its work with young people leads to increased critical thinking and tolerance, enhanced cultural exchange, and greater academic excellence.

IDEA provides resources and training to debate educators throughout the world and organizes international conferences and tournaments. The organization works with schools and universities, regional and national debate leagues, community groups, foundations, NGOs, businesses, and governments.

The collapse of the Soviet Union in 1991, and the subsequent disintegration of communist states in Central and Eastern Europe, promised economic growth, improved quality of life, and individual freedoms. However, antiquated methods of teaching, rooted in the notion that only one truth existed (that of the state), coupled with a lack of dialogue, underscored frustratingly slow progress and bred discontent among a generation of young people that had anticipated so much more.

In 1994, in an effort to stem this tide of apathy and push for a more rapid transition to democracy, the Open Society Institute (OSI [now Open Society Foundations]) launched its first network debate program. Although debate was an entirely new phenomenon to these countries, it provided an invaluable means for students to express opinions, to meet and discuss important issues, in short, to become informed citizens.

In 1999, IDEA was created (in the Netherlands) by OSI to coordinate these debate programs and act as an independent membership organization of national debate clubs, associations, programs, and individuals with the common goal of promoting mutual understanding and democracy globally by supporting discussion and active citizenship locally. Today, IDEA, through its various incarnations across the world, organizes debating activity in more than 60 languages in more than 50 countries. It continues to grow, striving constantly to improve the quality and quantity of its services—working locally, acting globally.

International Public Policy Forum (IPPF)—an international debating contest combining written advocacy and live debate performances on a public policy topic. Secondary schools throughout the world may enter the qualifying round, in which teams of debaters prepare an argumentative essay, backed by evidence that either affirms or negates that year's resolution. Judges choose the top 64 essays; those teams are then paired against one another in a series of written debates (an affirmative constructive is answered by a written negative constructive; each team then writes rebuttal papers). Judges read these papers and declare winners. The top eight teams then travel to New York City for a quarterfinal bracket of live debates; three-person teams compete in a modified Worlds Format Debate. The IPPF competition began in 2001; it is cosponsored by New York University and the Bickel and Brewer law firm.

interpretive events—dramatic contests, including dramatic interpretation, humorous interpretation, and duo interpretation; so called because the speaker is interpreting literature orally and with movement and gesture. Students may select readings from novels, short stories, stage plays, screen plays, or poetry, according to the requirement of the particular event. Some events permit the use of a manuscript; others require memorization. Interpretative events stress selection and editing of literature, vocal precision and variety, and expressive but appropriate physical delivery.

intrinsicness (American Policy Debate)—arguments are intrinsic if they are responses to the core of a proposal rather than its details. Consider an affirmative proposal that aims to reduce illegal immigration. A negative team might argue that an affirmative proposal is undesirable because it is carried out through a particular government agency or that its means of funding is unsuitable. The affirmative might respond that these are arguments against the method of implementation (which could be altered) and are not intrinsic—but that they are not arguments against reducing illegal immigration, which would be intrinsic.

intrinsicness permutation (American Policy Debate)— a permutation that tests the counterplan by including an element found in neither the affirmative plan nor the counterplan. For instance, if the affirmative plan argues that the federal government should implement an expanded program of early-childhood education, and the counterplan argues that state governments should do that instead, the affirmative might offer a permutation in which federal and state governments cooperate on a new program (cooperation being the new approach, which neither the plan nor the counterplan mentioned). Some critics consider intrinsicness permutations illegitimate because they constitute an actual shift in affirmative advocacy.

IPPF—*See* International Public Policy Forum

iron man (Parliamentary Debate, Worlds Format Debate)— a debater who competes alone in a two-person debate format and speaks in both positions, rather than just one. Iron man debaters are sometimes called "mavericks."

I-spec—*See* implementation specification

J

Jes Debate (Parliamentary Debate)—an Irish secondary school debate format, similar to British Parliamentary Debate, but with five speakers on each team and speeches limited to 4^1/$_2$ minutes.

judge panels—a number of individuals sitting as a panel to judge a debate. Elimination rounds at most debates and individual events tournaments are heard and evaluated by multiple judges, rather than by a single judge. Panels are always assigned in odd numbers. In most formats, members of the panel do not confer with one another before reaching decisions.

judging styles—*See* blank slate judging; critic-of-argument judging; games theory; skills judging

junior varsity—a competitive division one class below varsity, or championship, competition. Junior varsity debaters and speakers may have more than one year of experience, but are not yet considered ready to compete against the strongest and most experienced debaters. Many tournaments and leagues also offer novice divisions, which are generally restricted to competitors in their first year.

jurisdiction standard (American Policy Debate)—a topicality argument which argues that a debate judge may not endorse a proposal that falls outside the wording of the resolution. Jurisdiction arguments draw an analogy between the judge in the debate round and a judge in a courtroom, who would likewise be powerless to act on a case that did not fall under her jurisdiction, regardless of the merits of the case.

justification argument (American Policy Debate)—an argument claiming that the affirmative team must prove the necessity of all of the resolution and that they have failed to do so. Frequently, justification arguments, like topicality arguments, focus on particular words of the resolution; for instance, given a resolution that calls on the U.S. federal government to ban all military assistance to the Middle East, the negative might challenge the affirmative to justify banning "all" such assistance.

Karl Popper Debate—a form of debate often considered a good starting point for high school debaters. Devised by the Open Society Institute (now Open Society Foundations), it is promoted primarily as an educational tool to encourage critical thinking, tolerance for different views, and respect for ethical principles. *See* Appendix

kickout (American Policy Debate)—a strategic admission that a particular argument will no longer be advocated. A kickout usually includes an explanation of why the argument is no longer relevant to the debate and/or why the argument cannot be turned against the team that initiated it. For instance, a negative team might argue a spending disadvantage against the affirmative. The affirmative team may respond by saying that their plan does not require additional spending, but that, if it did, new spending would actually be good because it would revitalize the economy. A negative team's kickout would consist of granting that the plan does not require new spending and then pointing out that the affirmative's "new spending good" argument is now moot because no spending occurs.

Kritik (critique) (American Policy Debate)—an argument that challenges a fundamental philosophical assumption of an opponent's position. For example, a negative team might argue that an affirmative case that increases aid to developing nations should be rejected, despite its apparent advantages, because it is grounded in imperialist thinking.

An affirmative team might present a Kritik affirmative case that argues that the American education system is fundamentally capitalist and presents an alternative for the judge to endorse. Although Kritik structures vary, most will include:

- a link—identification of the argument, principle, or mindset within the affirmative case that the negative is criticizing (for example, the claim that state action is good or the assumption that capitalism is the correct economic system);

- an implication—explanation of why the affirmative's advocacy is harmful. The implication might include concrete impacts (capitalism causes war) or philosophical criticism (the affirmative assumes that humans are nature's masters rather than simply a part of nature's organism);

- an alternative—a competing course of action or mode of thought (we must replace nation-states with anarchy; we must reject humanist assumptions).

Types of Kritiks include:

- Kritiks of political ideas, including Kritiks of capitalism, Kritiks of state action (advocating anarchy), Kritiks of American race relations, and Kritiks of imperialism.

- Kritiks of philosophical concepts, including Kritiks of power relations based on the theories of Michel Foucault or Kritiks of the use of technology using the ideas of Martin Heidegger.

- Kritiks of discourse, which attack an opponent's use of language. These include objections to gendered language or language that demeans or misrepresents an ethnic or national group.

L

lag pairing—a form of power matching based on some, but not all, previous results. A "lag pair" of Round 4 might be based on the results from Rounds 1 and 2, but not Round 3. Lag pairing is generally used when time does not permit a full power pairing.

last shot—*See* final focus

lay judge—an individual who judges debates but is neither a coach nor former debater. Lay judges will most likely be concerned with the quality of a debater's speaking and reasoning rather than the intricacies of the topic or the technicalities of debate theory.

leader of the Opposition (LO) (British Parliamentary Debate, Parliamentary Debate)—the first speaker for the Opposition. The leader of the Opposition presents the initial response to the Government's case.

legislative intent (American Policy Debate)—a provision in a plan stating that future judgment of the meaning of the plan will be based on its advocate's speeches.

limited preparation events (Individual Events)—speaking competitions in which a contestant is presented with a topic and must quickly prepare a speech on it. The event tests students' ability to think and organize under pressure and to speak clearly and eloquently without notes or manuscript. The two most common limited preparation events are extemporaneous speaking (7-minute speeches on current issues, presented after 30 minutes' preparation time) and impromptu speaking (7 minutes divided between preparation and speaking time). Extemporaneous and impromptu speaking are the two major limited preparation events, but several other events—extemporaneous commentary, extemporaneous debate, and group discussion—are often offered in certain regions or as supplemental or novelty events at national tournaments. *See* extemporaneous commentary, extemporaneous debate, extemporaneous speaking, group discussion, impromptu speaking

Lincoln–Douglas Debate (LD)—a one-on-one debate that usually focuses on a proposition of value. *See* Appendix

linear impact (American Policy Debate)—a harmful result that occurs in proportion to action taken by an affirmative proposal. For instance, a negative team might argue that money spent on a large jobs program will increase inflation, with harm to the economy increasing in proportion to the amount of money spent.

line by line—refutation that answers each opposing argument in the order presented. This is distinct from an overview, which presents major concepts or broad themes of an opponent's refutation.

link—a connection between arguments. The term "link" most often refers to the connection between an affirmative team's advocacy and a negative disadvantage or Kritik argument. A negative team's economic disadvantage, for instance, might begin with "LINK—The affirmative plan requires substantial federal government spending."

link turnaround (American Policy Debate)—a reversal of an opponent's link argument. A negative disadvantage might claim that the affirmative plan angers China, leading to an increase in international tensions. A link turnaround would reverse the link, claiming that the plan actually pleases the Chinese leadership, thereby reducing the chance of increasing international tensions. Link turnarounds attempt to transform disadvantages into additional advantages for an affirmative team. Link turnarounds may also be applied to links to counterplans or Kritiks.

literal motion (Parliamentary Debate)—a Parliamentary Debate topic that suggests a specific course of action (as distinguished from metaphorical motions, which suggest many possible interpretations).

literature standard (American Policy Debate)—a means of judging whether an affirmative proposal meets the burden of topicality; if a search of key terms in the resolution produces books or articles discussing the affirmative proposal, it is reasonably topical. If the resolution calls on the affirmative to increase U.S. health care assistance to Africa, a search of keywords would probably generate discussion of infectious diseases, contraception, and family planning; it probably would not generate articles on veterinary care for lions or the benefits of transcendental meditation. The literature standard is a variant of the predictability standard, which argues that affirmative cases that a reasonable negative team could not predict as an example of the resolution should be excluded as non-topical.

loaded term—labeling a person or idea with a pejorative word or phrase. In a debate on Ukraine, for instance, references to "the Red menace" or "Russian expansionism" would be loaded terms, attempts to arouse Cold War–era anti-Russian sentiment.

locked—compelled to debate on a specific side in an elimination round. Generally, sides in an elimination round are decided by a flip of the coin, but when two teams have met previously in the tournament, they must reverse sides on their second meeting. (If Team A affirmed in the previous meeting, they must negate in the locked round, and vice versa.)

logos—one of Aristotle's basic rhetorical categories; logos refers to persuasion by the use of sound reasoning. Effective logos would include warranted claims, the use of appropriate examples and metaphors, and reference to well-chosen evidence.

long diagonal (Parliamentary Debate, Worlds University Debate)—the interaction between the Opening Government and Closing Opposition speakers.

longest standing (Congressional Debate)—a method of deciding which Congressional Debate speakers will be recognized. A presiding officer using the "longest standing" criterion would give priority to members who have waited longest to be recognized.

loose link (Parliamentary Debate)—a tournament that does not prescribe topics and allows the Government to choose the topic in any given round. "Loose link" also refers to a case that has only a vague or metaphorical relationship to the topic.

low-point win—an instance in which the decision and speaker points do not correlate; the winning team receives fewer speaker points than the losing team. Low-point wins are often given to teams with superior arguments but inferior speaking style or to teams who lose most arguments in the debate but have won one or two critical points.

Mace Debate (Parliamentary Debate)—a popular style of debate in British secondary schools. Two-person teams (affirmative, or proposition, and negative, or opposition) debate a resolution. The speaking order is as follows:

1st Proposition	7 minutes
1st Opposition	7 minutes
2nd Proposition	7 minutes
2nd Opposition	7 minutes

Debaters may present points of information (POIs).

After all four debaters have spoken, the debate is opened to the floor, and members of the audience may question the teams. After the floor debate, one speaker from each team (traditionally the first speaker), will speak for 4 minutes. In these summary speeches, the speaker typically answers the questions posed by the floor and any questions the opposition may have put forward before summarizing her own key points. Mace Debate emphasizes the use of analogy and example, organization, and persuasion of a general audience through deliberate, eloquent delivery.

magnitude—the size and scope of an impact, including the number of people killed or injured, money or jobs lost, property destroyed. Magnitude is one of the classic terms used by rebuttal speakers as they attempt to weigh the round. *See* decision calculus

mandate—the section of an affirmative plan that sets out what the affirmative wants to see put into action.

manner (Parliamentary Debate, World Schools Debate)—the style, structure, and presentation quality of a debate speech. Manner includes eye contact, voice modulation, hand gestures, and clever or vivid use of language. It is distinct from matter or the content of the argument.

matter (Parliamentary Debate, World Schools Debate)—the content of an argument presented in a debate speech, including the validity of its premises, support through evidence or example, and clear explanation of the importance of the argument in the context of the debate round. It is distinct from manner, or the style and presentation quality of the argument.

maverick—a lone debater competing in a two-person debate event. Maverick debating is usually the result of sudden illness or emergency that has forced the withdrawal of one partner. Some tournaments do not permit mavericks, even in an emergency; other tournaments may not permit mavericks to advance to elimination rounds. Sometimes called an "iron man."

member of the Government (MG) (British Parliamentary Debate, Parliamentary Debate)—in American Parliamentary Debate, the second speaker for the Government; in British Parliamentary Debate, the third speaker.

member of the Opposition (MO) (British Parliamentary Debate, Parliamentary Debate)—in American Parliamentary Debate, the second speaker for the Opposition; in British Parliamentary Debate, the third speaker.

metaphorical motion (Parliamentary Debate)—a Parliamentary Debate topic that suggests multiple substantive interpretations. For example, teams debating "That this House should wake up and smell the coffee" might interpret the motion as a demand for stronger national defense, a call for more responsible budgeting decisions, or a more general plea for realism and self-awareness.

method (Parliamentary Debate)—a team's response to the dynamics of a given debate. Method includes each speaker's ability to communicate or signpost a pattern to the judge, correct identification of major (as opposed to minor or tangential) arguments, the effectiveness of a team's time allocation, and the structure and strategic effectiveness of the case that is originally presented.

method of agreement (Karl Popper Debate)—a method of reasoning used in cause-and-effect analysis that examines more than one case where two elements are simultaneously present, concluding that one is the cause of the other.

method of correlation (Karl Popper Debate)—a method of reasoning used in cause-and-effect analysis that examines examples that demonstrate that as the amount of the cause increases (or decreases), the effect will also increase (or decrease).

method of difference (Karl Popper Debate)—a method of reasoning used in cause-and-effect analysis that examines examples wherein both the purported cause and the purported effect are absent, concluding that one is the cause of the other.

middle school forensics—competitive speech and debate activities for U.S. students in grades 6 through 8. Middle school competition has been modeled and nurtured by the National Junior Forensic League (an extension of the National Speech and Debate Association, formerly the National Forensic League) and has grown immensely in the past 15 years. Additionally, some state and Urban Debate League organizations offer middle school competition, and an increasing number of summer debate workshops offer middle school divisions. Along with most debate events, offerings generally include original oratory, dramatic interpretation, poetry interpretation, prose interpretation, storytelling, and informative speaking.

minor repair (American Policy Debate)—a strategy in which the negative team suggests that an acceleration of current policy trends could gain the affirmative advantage. A minor repair argument must establish a trend toward solvency in the present system and must show an existing mechanism that might accomplish change. For instance, an affirmative team might argue that the U.S. government needs different laws and new agencies if it is to properly repair bridges and roads; a negative minor repair might argue that Congress would like to repair bridges and roads and that current agencies are adequate—only the "minor repair" of more money is necessary. A minor repair is distinct from a counterplan, which contends that the present system is inadequate and proposes major programmatic change.

mitigation—arguments that reduce the harm claimed by the opposing team. An affirmative team proposing a program of bridge and road repair might claim to save 10,000 lives each year; the negative might offer counterevidence indicating the number would be only 5,000. Mitigation arguments serve to reduce the opposing team's advantage or disadvantage impact, making it easier to outweigh that impact with one's own.

mixed interpretation (Individual Events)—a competitive event in which a contestant presents a set of brief cuttings from two or more different genres of literature (prose, poetry, or drama) that express a theme. The program should develop the theme through the use of narrative, evocative language, and vocal characterization. A substantial portion of the total time must be devoted to each of the genres used in the program. The use of a manuscript is required. Maximum time is 10 minutes, including introduction. Mixed interpretation is sometimes called "program oral interpretation."

MJP—*See* mutual judge preferences

Mock Trial—a competitive event in which students assume the roles of attorneys and witnesses in a courtroom proceeding. *See* Appendix

model (Parliamentary Debate)—in Australia-Asia Debate, a plan or proposal offered by the affirmative or Government team in support of the resolution.

Moot Court—an extracurricular activity at many law schools in which participants take part in simulated court proceedings, which usually involve drafting briefs and participating in oral argument. Moot Court in law school differs from a high school or collegiate Mock Trial, as "moot court" usually refers to a simulated civil appellate case, while "mock trial" usually refers to a simulated jury or bench trial. Moot Court does not involve actual testimony by witnesses or the presentation of evidence; it is focused solely on the application of the law to a common set of evidentiary assumptions to which the competitors must be introduced. In most countries, the phrase "a moot court" may be shortened to simply "a moot" and the activity may be called "mooting."

motion (British Parliamentary Debate, Parliamentary Debate)—the proposition or resolution to be debated in any given round.

mutual exclusivity (American Policy Debate)—a standard for judging the competitiveness of a counterplan. If it would be physically or logically impossible to implement both the affirmative plan and the negative counterplan at the same time, then the plan and counterplan are mutually exclusive. For instance, if the plan calls for an increased minimum wage, and the counterplan calls for a decreased minimum wage, the two proposals are mutually exclusive.

mutual judge preferences (MJP)—a system of tournament judge assignment. Teams and their coaches are presented with an advance list of judges; they then indicate through categorical ratings or ordinal rankings which judges they value (or do not value). At most national circuit tournaments, the judges in the varsity pool are ranked beforehand from 1 to 5 by the debaters and their coaches as part of the mutual judge preference system. A 1 is the best possible ranking; a 5 is a judge with a conflict of interest regarding that team; and a 6 is a "strike"—one who may never judge the debater. Teams are usually allowed a limited number of strikes per tournament. During the tournament, the tabulation staff will attempt to give each round a mutually preferred judge (i.e., a judge who is designated as a 1 for both sides). Different debaters and coaches will "pref" (prefer) different judges depending on their past experiences with those judges and the argument preferences the judges have expressed.

narrative—an approach to advocacy that breaks from traditional propositional argument and emphasizes storytelling and personal testimony as a persuasive tool. A narrative case might replace statistics and the conclusions of experts with the descriptive language of persons affected by the harms under discussion—or even the personal reflections of the debater herself. Such a case usually includes framework arguments claiming unique advantages for narrative as argument.

National Association of Urban Debate Leagues (NAUDL)—a nonprofit organization that promotes and supports urban debate leagues throughout the United States. NAUDL sees urban debate as a powerful tool that prepares low-income students of color to succeed in college and in their future careers. NAUDL assists local urban leagues as they organize and support competitive debate teams in urban public schools across the country. The assistance occurs in three major ways. First, NAUDL engages in fund-raising on behalf of the 19 Urban Debate Leagues, which serve more than 500 high schools and middle schools across the United States; funds come from corporations, foundations, and individual donors. Second, NAUDL conducts research and planning that guides the growth of urban leagues; its strategic plan seeks to triple the number of urban debaters by 2019. NAUDL research also provides valuable data proving the positive educational impact of urban debate in terms of increased test scores, higher graduation rates, and lower dropout rates. Third, NAUDL provides curricular and coaching resources for new debaters and coaches.

Since 2008, NAUDL has sponsored a national championship tournament in policy debate for urban debaters. NAUDL funding allows the strongest debaters from each of the 19 Urban Debate Leagues to travel to the tournament, all expenses paid, for three and a half days of competition, instruction, and socializing. The tournament coincides with NAUDL's annual fund-raising dinner. *See also* urban debate leagues

National Catholic Forensics League (NCFL)—an American speech and debate league formed in 1951. It is organized into more than 60 local leagues whose borders correspond roughly to Roman Catholic dioceses. Any public, parochial, or private school may join NCFL, although each league must have at least one Catholic high school in its membership. Each league sends qualifying speakers and debaters to the NCFL Grand National Speech and Debate Tournament, which is held annually over Memorial Day weekend.

National Christian Forensics and Communication Association (NCFCA)—a speech and debate league for Christian homeschooled students in the United States. With nearly 7,000 competitors, the NCFCA is the third-largest forensics league in the nation. NCFCA is governed by a national board of directors, with regional and state leaders coordinating various tournaments throughout the season. Tournaments are run by volunteers—generally parents or club directors and league officials in the area. The judging pool includes parents of competitors, NCFCA alumni, NCFCA coaches, and members of the community.

NCFCA sponsors 10 regional tournaments, held in April or early May, where students may qualify for the NCFCA national tournament held each June. The tournament offers competition in individual events, including after-dinner speaking, informative speaking, persuasive speaking, duo interpretation, humorous interpretation, extemporaneous speaking, and impromptu speaking. Additionally, NCFCA offers Policy and Lincoln–Douglas debate divisions. Students may compete in as many as five different individual events and one debate event.

National Debate Tournament (NDT)—one of two national championship tournaments for American college policy debate. It was first held in 1947 at the U.S. Military Academy. Since 1967, it has been held at a different host university each year. Teams may qualify for the NDT in several ways. First, the NDT committee selects a "first round" of 16 teams that it regards as the best in the nation. Then, each of the nine NDT districts holds a qualifying contest; another 46 teams proceed to NDT as district qualifiers. Finally, the NDT committee chooses another 16 "second round" teams among those not yet qualified to fill out the tournament. No school may qualify more than three teams to the NDT.

NDT shares a year-long topic and most tournament rules with the other major college national championship, CEDA Nationals, but each tournament has distinctive features. NDT qualification is extremely selective; CEDA Nationals has no qualifying procedure or limit on the number of teams a school can bring. Additionally, NDT is more identified with traditional policy debate, while CEDA Nationals is regarded as more welcoming to Kritik argument and other nontraditional approaches.

National Educational Debate Association (NEDA)—an intercollegiate debate organization that emphasizes audience-friendly, evidence-based debate on policy and value resolutions. It was founded in 1994 by debate educators who had participated in the Cross Examination Debate Association (CEDA), but felt that CEDA debate was no longer teaching good communication practices. NEDA schedules eight invitational tournaments a year, primarily in the U.S. Midwest. The association's members select two resolutions for each academic year—a fall semester policy resolution and a spring semester value resolution.

Judges at NEDA tournaments may, on occasion, award losses to both teams in rounds where debaters are speaking too quickly or engaging in excessively technical argument. By design, half of the judges at any NEDA tournament are lay judges.

National Forensic Association (NFA)—an intercollegiate organization designed to promote excellence in individual events and debate. Since 1971, the NFA has sponsored NFA Nationals, the first national intercollegiate tournament for individual events. NFA individual events include extemporaneous speaking, impromptu speaking, persuasive speaking, informative speaking, rhetorical criticism, after-dinner speaking, prose interpretation, poetry interpretation, and duo interpretation of drama. In 2008, NFA added dramatic interpretation to its offerings.

NFA schools also compete in Lincoln–Douglas Debate. Their format differs from high school Lincoln–Douglas; NFA–LD is evidence-based policy debate, and, like high school policy debate, it uses one topic for the entire academic year. Rather than support general ideas or values, affirmative competitors propose a particular policy to adopt as a representation of the resolution. Negative competitors will generally attempt to either demonstrate a lack of need for that policy or argue that its disadvantages outweigh its benefits.

National Forensic League (NFL)—*See* National Speech and Debate Association

National Invitational Tournament of Champions (NITOC)—a national speech and debate tournament for Christian homeschooled students. The tournament is sponsored by Stoa USA, a national organization devoted to Christian homeschool forensics. The NITOC offers Parliamentary, Lincoln–Douglas, and policy debate divisions, as well as competition in 12 individual events. Students qualify for the NITOC by excelling in state and local homeschool tournaments. Six hundred thirty students from around the United States attended the 2014 NITOC, making it the largest tournament of its kind.

National Junior Forensic League (NJFL)—an affiliate of the National Speech and Debate Association (NSDA, formerly National Forensic League) that organizes and promotes speech and debate competition among middle schools. NJFL offers middle school students and teachers a range of services comparable to that offered to high schools by NSDA. NJFL provides an honorary society for middle school competitors, with recognition at various levels of outstanding competitive achievement. It also provides a wide range of educational materials (online, print, and video) for students and coaches. Finally, NJFL sponsors a national tournament, open to U.S. and international middle school students, run during the NSDA national tournament. The NJFL tournament offers policy,

Lincoln–Douglas, Congressional, and Public Forum debate, as well as a range of individual events. Participation has grown steadily since the league's founding in 1999; more than 1,000 students attended the 2014 NJFL tournament.

National Parliamentary Debate Association (NPDA)—the larger of the two national intercollegiate parliamentary debate organizations in the United States. (The American Parliamentary Debate Association [APDA] is the other.) Its membership is national, with participating schools on both coasts and throughout the country. NPDA tournaments issue a new topic each round, generally in areas such as politics, philosophy, and current affairs, with speeches beginning after limited preparation time. The NPDA sanctions tournaments throughout the nation and gives year-long sweepstakes awards based on performance at these sanctioned tournaments. It also runs the NPDA Championship Tournament—held in late March or early April at rotating host sites.

NPDA debate differs from APDA debate in two important ways. First, NPDA topics are more likely to be grounded in politics and current affairs, while APDA topics are more likely to lend themselves to philosophical or even humorous approaches. Second, many NPDA rounds have come to resemble American policy debate, featuring rapid rates of speech and reliance on technical argument forms such as Kritiks and counterplans. Although both associations have members throughout the United States, APDA schools are concentrated in the Eastern United States, and NPDA schools are more likely to be found in the West.

National Speech and Debate Association (NSDA)—formerly the National Forensic League, the NSDA is the oldest and largest high school speech and debate association in the United States. Since its founding in 1925, it has enrolled more than 1.4 million students. The association has several functions. First, it is an educational honor society, designed to recognize and motivate high school students who become proficient in public speaking. Competing speakers and debaters accumulate award points and receive NSDA honors based on their success at tournaments. Second, the NSDA hosts the nation's preeminent national high school tournament each June. Students qualify for NSDA Nationals through superior performance at more than 100 district tournaments throughout the nation. Additionally, the association sponsors a middle school national tournament through its affiliate organization, the National Junior Forensic League. Finally, the NSDA models forensic activity nationwide. The NSDA executive committee sets rules for most debate and speech events; NSDA wording committees develop the topics for Lincoln–Douglas and Public Forum debate. NSDA also promotes forensics education through its many instructional publications and videos.

naturalistic fallacy—originally, the claim that qualities or conditions found in nature are inherently good or right; more recently, that existing policies are necessarily good. Variations on this fallacy are often found in debates about current affairs ("Most developed nations have some form of socialized medicine; therefore, it must be successful." "If people really thought that stronger gun control was necessary, we would have it.").

NAUDL—*See* National Association of Urban Debate Leagues

NCFCA—*See* National Christian Forensics and Communication Association

NCFL—*See* National Catholic Forensics League

NDT Debate—a style of American Policy Debate characterized by rapid delivery and exhaustive research on a broad national topic. *See also* National Debate Tournament

NEDA—*See* National Educational Debate Association

need-plan case (American Policy Debate)—a traditional style of affirmative case in which the affirmative identifies a deficiency in the present system and offers a plan that meets that need. Generally, need-plan cases address relatively small problems and claim to solve them completely. Need-plan cases are rarely heard today outside extremely traditional circuits.

negation theory (American Policy Debate)—the notion that the negative's only burden is to prove the resolution untrue. The negative may win by negating any of the stock issues (harm, inherency, solvency), by winning a disadvantage or Kritik, or by presenting a competitive alternative. Negative positions need not be consistent, they may even be contradictory as long as they negate the resolution.

negative block (American Policy Debate)—the second negative constructive and first negative rebuttal speeches, taken together, form the negative block—13 minutes of time for negative argument, interrupted only by the cross-examination period that follows the second negative constructive. An effective negative team will split extension of the issues presented in the first negative constructive between the two speeches of the negative block. The block is considered one major structural advantage of debating on the negative, because the first affirmative rebuttalist has only 5 minutes to refute 13 minutes of opposing argument. (The affirmative, however, has the first speech, the last speech, and the right to choose the arguments that begin the round.)

negative fiat (American Policy Debate)—the negative's assumed power to put its own proposal (counterplan) into effect. The extent of negative fiat is a subject of controversy. Most coaches and judges agree that the negative team may propose action by an agent other than the federal government, including an international actor. Questions arise when the negative attempts to enact a proposal through an agent of government that does not yet exist (e.g., world government) or through multiple governments. Negative fiat power is not necessarily limited to the scope of the resolution, but it is limited to subjects of legal or government power.

net benefits (American Policy Debate)—a way of proving that a counterplan is *competitive*; in other words, that the counterplan is not merely a good idea but a reason to reject the affirmative proposal. A counterplan has net benefits if adopting a counterplan alone would be superior to adopting the counterplan and the affirmative plan together. Net benefits may take the form of an advantage accrued by the counterplan, but not by the plan, or of a disadvantage that occurs as a result of the affirmative proposal, but not as a result of the counterplan. For instance, the affirmative might propose a federal government program to repair roads and bridges. A negative team might propose a counterplan in which the 50 state governments undertake those repairs, together with a spending disadvantage (arguing that increased federal spending at this time would injure the economy). Since the affirmative plan has a disadvantage, but the counterplan does not, the counterplan is net beneficial.

new argument—an argument presented in a rebuttal speech that has no antecedent in a constructive speech. New arguments are considered to be illegitimate, particularly if a team presents them in their last rebuttal. New arguments should not be confused with extensions or elaborations of arguments that have already been initiated in constructive speeches or answers to arguments made in the previous speech by the opposing team. Additionally, new evidence in support of arguments that have already been presented is permitted in rebuttal speeches.

NFA—*See* National Forensic Association

NITOC—*See* National Invitational Tournament of Champions

NJFL—*See* National Junior Forensic League

non sequitur (Latin for "it does not follow")—an argument in which the conclusion is disconnected from the premise. It can also refer to refutation that is totally unresponsive to the original argument. ("My opponent argues that our plan will cause taxes to rise. Our response is that the plan will reduce water pollution.")

normal means (American Policy Debate)—the usual methods government uses to implement legislation. Affirmative plans generally contain language indicating that the plan will use "normal means" for funding and enforcement.

North American Debating Championship (NorthAms)—the official university parliamentary debate championship of North America sanctioned by the American Parliamentary Debate Association and the Canadian University Society for Intercollegiate Debate. NorthAms is held annually, with the United States and Canada alternating as hosts.

novice—a beginning speaker or debater. In high school competitions, a novice is generally understood to be a speaker in his or her first year, though some leagues may define novice status in terms of number of tournaments attended. College tournaments generally define novice as "first year of college competition," though debaters with significant high school experience are usually discouraged from entering novice divisions.

NPDA—*See* National Parliamentary Debate Association

NSDA—*See* National Speech and Debate Association

null and void clause (Congressional Debate)—language included in any bill that supersedes or overrides existing legislation.

object fiat (American Policy Debate)—an attempt to enact change through the subject of the resolution, rather than its agent. Object fiat is usually attempted by the negative team on topics involving foreign policy. For instance, if the topic required the affirmative to substantially change U.S. foreign policy toward China, and the affirmative team argued that the United States should pressure China to change its human rights policies, the negative team might argue that the Chinese should change their policies instead. Object fiat is generally regarded as an illegitimate debate tactic, because it shifts debate away from the question posed by the resolution (How should U.S foreign policy change?).

observation—a descriptive conclusion or assumption, usually part of a prepared case. Observations differ from contentions because they are usually general or theoretical in nature, standing apart from the rest of the case. They often provide criteria for the judge to use in her decision ("We begin with an observation: the negative team must defend the status quo.") or attempt to limit the scope of the debate ("We have one observation: foreign policy is distinct from economic or military policy.").

octafinal round—an elimination round consisting of 16 teams, 8 of which would proceed to the quarterfinal round.

off-case arguments—arguments presented by the negative team that do not directly refute the affirmative advantages or stock issues. Off-case arguments include disadvantages, counterplans, Kritiks, topicality, and other theory arguments. Debaters frequently use the term as they introduce their speeches ("I'll have three off-case arguments, and then I'll go on-case.").

on-case arguments—arguments that directly refute the affirmative's inherency, harms, advantages, or solvency. Debaters frequently use the term as they introduce their speeches ("I'll begin with four off-case arguments before going on-case.") ("I'll have three off-case arguments, and then I'll go on-case.")

online debating—debates conducted via the Internet using email, video, or a combination of both media. Debaters generally observe word and/or time limits, but have days or perhaps weeks to prepare responses to arguments and are able to do additional research as the online round develops. Online debating eliminates the barrier of travel costs and is an especially useful format for debaters who wish to compete internationally.

open cross-examination (American Policy Debate)—in policy debate, a question-and-answer period in which all speakers may participate. Generally, one debater conducts most of the questioning of the debater who has just completed a constructive speech, but "open" cross-examination permits the debaters' partners to assist with answers or pose their own questions if they desire. Some traditional tournament formats discourage or forbid open cross-examination.

open division—a division of competition that has no restrictions on participation.

open-ended question—a query that allows the respondent to answer at length. Questioners should generally avoid open-ended questions because they give respondents the opportunity to elaborate on a position, offer a new argument, or simply run out the clock.

opp-choice case (Parliamentary Debate)—a case in which the Government presents a topic to the Opposition and allows them to choose which side to defend. The Opposition is granted some preparation time to consider the choice. For instance, the Government might offer the topic "Is targeted killing morally justified?" and allow the Opposition to decide whether they prefer negating or affirming. Occasionally, more than two choices are offered ("Should we be communists, socialists, or capitalists?"); the Opposition would select first, and the Government would then claim one of the remaining options.

Opposition (Parliamentary Debate)—the team that opposes the motion; the negative team in a Parliamentary Debate.

Opposition whip (OW) (British Parliamentary Debate)— the last Opposition speaker. The whip summarizes the Opposition's position and answers the Government whip.

opposition wins—the total number of wins awarded to a team's opponents in the course of a tournament. When speaker points are tied among teams with the same win-loss record, opposition wins is one tie-breaking instrument used to decide tournament seeds and speaker awards.

oral critique—a post-round discussion initiated by the judge. Oral critiques usually include an announcement of the judge's decision, together with the reasons for the decision and additional suggestions regarding style and content. Some debate tournaments, such as the National Catholic Forensics League, restrict judges to written comments and do not permit oral critiques or disclosure of decisions.

oratorical interpretation (Individual Events)—a competitive Individual Event in which a contestant presents a speech written by another. The speaker may choose a historic speech given by a famous public figure, a contemporary speech given at a commencement or memorial, or even a successful speech written for tournament competition. The speech is memorized and rehearsed. Oratorical interpretation is rarely offered by college tournaments and is often used as a training event for middle school and younger high school competitors. Oratorical interpretation is sometimes known as "declamation."

original oratory (Individual Events)—a competitive high school Individual Event in which students deliver an original persuasive or inspirational speech. The speech may attempt to change an audience's attitude on a public issue (why we need stronger gun control legislation), or it may simply move the audience to reconsider personal values and practices (why we need to resist the intrusion of technology into our daily lives). Original oratories may quote a limited number of words from other sources, but the speech should be the student's own work. The speech is memorized and rehearsed; generally, 10 minutes is the maximum length. In college competitions, original oratory is usually called "persuasion" or "persuasive speaking."

original poetry (Individual Events)—a competitive event, similar to poetry interpretation, except that the poetry is the student's own work. This event is offered by some state leagues and college tournaments.

O-spec—*See* overspecification

ought (Lincoln–Douglas Debate)—the usual verb in Lincoln–Douglas value resolutions, generally understood to imply moral obligation as opposed to mere desirability. For instance, a resolution phrased as "Nations ought to ban capital punishment" would indicate that nations are morally bound to enact a ban; "Nations should ban capital punishment" would indicate that nations would derive benefits from a ban.

overspecification (O-spec) (American Policy Debate)— a negative argument claiming that the affirmative plan has illegitimately chosen to defend action by a particular subset of the federal government rather than the entire federal government. For example, "The affirmative plan states that their plan to rebuild roads and bridges will be undertaken by the Army Corps of Engineers. This is an abuse of their fiat power, since the resolution does not indicate any particular agency and because they have chosen that agency in an attempt to fund their plan via the military budget, depriving us of our funding arguments."

overview—a brief synthesis of the issues under discussion, offered at the beginning of a rebuttal speech. An overview contrasts with line-by-line discussion, in which each particular argument is answered systematically and in order.

P

panacea (Worlds Debate)—a term applied to a case that makes unrealistic claims.

paperless debate—an increasingly prevalent practice in which speeches, briefs, evidence, and other documents are available only on laptops. Judges and opponents who wish to examine material do so by looking at the debater's computer screen or the materials are transferred via flash drives.

Paris-style debating (Parliamentary Debate)—a type of Parliamentary Debate used exclusively in France. Five-person teams debate for and against a resolution. Proposition (affirmative) and Opposition (negative) speakers alternate, and each debater speaks for 6 minutes. In other respects, the format is similar to British Parliamentary Debate.

Parliamentary Debate—a style of debate competition very loosely based on the traditions of the British Parliament and most often conducted at the college or university level. Parliamentary Debate (or "parli") is very popular throughout the English-speaking world and is the model for other international debate formats. *See* Appendix

pathos—one of Aristotle's basic rhetorical categories. Pathos refers to appeals to the audience's emotions, with the goal of arousing their sympathies and imagination. Appeals from pathos might include the use of sad or alarming examples and narratives that make the problem under discussion concrete and personal. Figurative language and sensory detail are frequently employed.

pentathlon (Individual Events)—a special award category for speakers who enter five or more events at one tournament.

performance—an approach to advocacy that breaks from traditional propositional argument and emphasizes music, poetry, and dramatic presentation as modes of persuasion. A performance case might replace statistics and the conclusions of experts with live or recorded musical performances or dramatic presentations that express attitudes about the issues under discussion. Such cases usually include arguments claiming unique advantages for performance as argument.

permutation (American Policy Debate)—an affirmative argument that attempts to demonstrate that a negative counterplan or Kritik is not a reason to reject the affirmative proposal. Consider an affirmative plan that increases federal funding for public education. The negative might argue that education issues are best addressed by state governments, rather than by the federal government, and propose a counterplan in which state governments increase their funding. The affirmative's permutation argument might be that increases from both levels of government would be useful, but that the desirability of increased state funding does not negate the desirability of increased federal funding. If the negative were to offer a Kritik of capitalism—saying that public education is simply a tool of capitalist indoctrination—the affirmative could argue that we could still increase funding while offering an anticapitalist curriculum. Types of permutations include:

- *intrinsicness permutations*, which test the counterplan by including an element found in neither the affirmative plan nor the counterplan. For instance, if the affirmative plan argues that the federal government should implement an expanded program of early-childhood education, and the counterplan argues that state governments should do that instead, the affirmative might offer a permutation in which federal and state governments cooperate on a new program (cooperation being the new approach, which neither the plan nor the counterplan mentioned). Some critics consider intrinsicness permutations illegitimate, because they constitute an actual shift in affirmative advocacy.

- *severance permutations*, which test the counterplan by arguing that a part of the plan (but not the entire plan) competes with the counterplan. Assume an affirmative plan in which the U.S. federal government establishes and funds a road and bridge repair program; the negative counterplans with 50-state action. The affirmative argues a permutation in which the states fund a federally administered program, thereby severing the funding portion of their original plan. Many judges regard severance permutations as an unfair shift in advocacy.

- *time frame permutations* test the counterplan by arguing that the plan and counterplan need not be done simultaneously and that doing one before the other could achieve the net benefits that the counterplan claims. For instance, the negative might advocate a state's counterplan that claims a disadvantage to federal government action *at the present time* as part of a claim of net benefits; the affirmative might respond by saying that we could do state action now and federal government action later.

persuasive speaking (Individual Events)—a competitive high school Individual Event in which students deliver an original persuasive or inspirational speech. The speech may attempt to change an audience's attitude on a public issue (why we need stronger gun control legislation), or it may simply move the audience to reconsider personal values and practices (why we need to resist the intrusion of technology into our daily lives). Persuasive speeches may quote a limited number of words from other sources, but the speech should be the student's own work. The speech is memorized and rehearsed; generally, 10 minutes is the maximum length. In high school competitions, persuasive speaking is usually called "original oratory."

PIC—*See* plan inclusive counterplan

Pi Kappa Delta—an American college and university honorary society for educators, students, and alumni who are involved in competitive forensics. Pi Kappa Delta takes its name from the first three letters of a Greek phrase ("The art of persuasion, beautiful and just"). The society began in 1911 as a confederation of debating organizations in small Midwestern colleges. Pi Kappa Delta sponsored the first national forensics tournaments, beginning in 1919. Today Pi Kappa Delta sponsors the annual National Comprehensive Tournament, which includes American Forensic Association Individual Events and several debate events, including college-level Lincoln–Douglas and Public Forum debate. The society also maintains an active scholarship program, sponsors a journal, and funds projects that enhance speech and debate pedagogy. Pi Kappa

Delta is considered a forerunner of the National Speech and Debate Association (formerly the National Forensic League), with which it retains close ties.

plan (American Policy Debate)—a formal, binding, comprehensive statement by the affirmative of a policy action that implements the resolution. At minimum, a plan includes an *agent* (who or what will do the plan) and the *mandates* (what is to be done). Plans may consist of legislation, increased or decreased government regulation, executive action, a court decision, or combinations of all these. Plan language is usually precise but brief and does not always explicitly describe details such as funding and enforcement, but, if questioned, the affirmative speakers must provide explanations of these details. Most affirmative plans are modeled on existing legislative proposals or academic studies; accordingly, affirmative teams defend the measures outlined in those documents.

plan focus (American Policy Debate)—the idea that the debate should focus on an example of the resolution rather than on the resolution itself. In policy debate, for instance, the affirmative team would not defend "that the U.S. government should increase economic engagement with Latin America" as a general principle; in an individual debate round, they might propose that the United States remove its trade embargo against Cuba or promote free trade with Colombia. Plan focus is widely accepted in policy debate, but is quite controversial in Lincoln–Douglas and Public Forum debate. Debaters who advocate for plan focus might argue that debating the resolution as a general statement produces shallow debates or that, since time constraints prevent full discussion of the many aspects of a resolution, limiting discussion to one example is best.

plan inclusive counterplan (PIC) (American Policy Debate)—a negative proposal that includes substantial parts of the affirmative proposal. Examples would include delay counterplans, which advocate enacting the affirmative plan at a later time; exclusion counterplans, which advocate the affirmative plan minus certain provisions; and consultation counterplans, which only enact the affirmative plan after consultation with other governments. Many affirmative teams argue that PICs are illegitimate, because they offer only minor variations on the affirmative proposal and therefore are not truly "negative" proposals.

plan meet need (American Policy Debate)—a negative argument claiming that the affirmative's proposal will be unable to solve the problem. Plan meet need arguments are essentially traditional solvency arguments, usually focusing on the actual mechanics of the plan. If the affirmative proposes an ambitious solar power research and development program, the negative might argue that there are not yet enough properly trained specialists to staff such a program; therefore, the plan will be unable to meet the need.

plan side (American Policy Debate)—the portion of the debate devoted to topicality, disadvantages, counterplans, and Kritiks; as distinct from case side, which is devoted to arguments on harm, significance, inherency, and solvency.

platform events (Individual Events)—oratorical contests, including original oratory, persuasive speaking, after-dinner speaking, and expository or informative speaking; so called because they might be delivered from a platform or dais. These speeches are researched, written, and memorized by the competitors; only a limited number of quoted words are permitted. Platform events stress vocal fluency, expressive physical delivery, and precise, evocative use of language. *See* after-dinner speaking, expository speaking, original oratory, persuasive speaking

PMRE—*See* Prime Minister's Rebuttal Extension

poetry interpretation (Individual Events)—an oral interpretation event in which contestants prepare a 10-minute program of excerpts from one or more poems and deliver the program from a manuscript. The focus may be on the development of a theme—more likely if several poems are included—or the focus may be on highlighting images and language use or, occasionally, the voice of a character. Poetry interpretation is a standard event at college Individual Events tournaments and is sometimes offered at high school tournaments.

POI—*See* point of information

point of clarification (British Parliamentary Debate, Parliamentary Debate)—questions asked by the Opposition as the Government is presenting the specifics of its case. ("How exactly will the Government enforce the proposal?" "Will the Government assign only men to combat roles or women also?")

point of information (POI) (British Parliamentary Debate, Parliamentary Debate)—a short question or statement put to a speaker on the opposing side, which he must respond to directly. Points of information are designed to forward the cause of the person applying for the POI. They can challenge a speaker's argument, point out an apparent contradiction, or highlight a point that the interrupter intends to make in her speech. Points of information are taken at the discretion of the debater holding the floor.

point of order (British Parliamentary Debate, Parliamentary Debate)—an interjection made by the Opposition when the speaker is introducing a new argument during a rebuttal speech or grossly mischaracterizing arguments. During a point of order, official time (usually kept by the judge) is stopped while the judge listens and considers the point raised.

point of personal privilege (British Parliamentary Debate, Parliamentary Debate)—an objection made when the speaker makes offensive claims or personal attacks. Time is stopped while the judge considers the objection.

policy making (American Policy Debate)—a role-playing theory that posits debaters and judges as participants in a government policy-making process. Policy-making debate mimics government processes, especially legislative processes, and concerns itself with the details of implementation. Policy making tends to assume a utilitarian calculus in which a judge operates within a plan focus (not a resolutional focus) and weighs the benefits of an affirmative proposal versus disadvantages.

political capital—a politician's ability to influence a policy outcome. Political capital may include an ability to grant or withhold favors, personal popularity with the electorate, or simple respect.

political capital disadvantage (American Policy Debate)—a negative argument that claims that the affirmative plan should not be adopted because the political cost of legislative enactment of the plan is unacceptable.

Generally, negative teams argue that the president must always use his power and influence to ensure passage of a controversial proposal and that passing the plan sacrifices political capital necessary to get other, arguably more important, policies passed. For instance, some commentators opposed enactment of Pres. Barack Obama's health care plan because it expended political capital that might have been better applied to proposals that created greater advantages, such as economic stimulus or immigration reform.

politics disadvantage (American Policy Debate)—a popular negative argument that claims that passage of the affirmative plan will trigger an unfortunate chain of political events, culminating in harm that outweighs the affirmative advantage. The most common version of a politics disadvantage supposes that the plan, if enacted in the real world, would cause resentment or conflict that would make the achievement of other, more desirable goals, less likely; therefore, the plan *should not* be adopted because its unintended consequences will outweigh any good it might accomplish. For instance, an affirmative proposal that creates new jobs for poor people might anger conservative Republicans in Congress and make them unlikely to support critical foreign policy measures that (the negative might argue) are necessary to reduce the risk of war.

The affirmative has a number of responses to claims of politics disadvantages. First, the affirmative might argue that the debate should center on the desirability of the plan rather than the details and side effects of its implementation. Second, the affirmative can contest negative claims about how the plan is perceived by citizens or legislators; they might try to prove that the plan would be well-received rather than poorly received. Third, the affirmative could argue that the impact of the disadvantage is not unique or not a direct outcome of the affirmative proposal; that conservative Republicans would not support the foreign policy measures in question whether or not the affirmative plan is adopted. Finally, the affirmative might attempt to turn the impact of the disadvantage, arguing that congressional support for the foreign policy measures in question would, in fact, increase, not decrease, the risk of war.

post-fiat implication (American Policy Debate)—reasons why government actors (or other policy makers) should adopt the philosophy set forth in a negative Kritik argument. For instance, the negative might present a Kritik of capitalism, saying that the affirmative's proposal to build new roads and bridges simply perpetuates an unacceptable economic structure. They would give reasons why the judge should reject capitalism and ask the judge to vote negative for those reasons.

post hoc ergo propter hoc (after this, therefore because of this)—fallacy that confuses sequence with causation. ("I let my sister use my car for a week. The day after she returned it, the transmission failed. My sister ruined my car.")

power matching—a method of organizing tournament competition. A power-matched tournament attempts to pair teams of similar strength against each other in each round based on ongoing results. After two or three randomly paired rounds, teams are matched with opponents with the same win-loss records. This process continues, round by round, until the preliminary rounds are concluded.

power pairing—*See* power matching

predictability standard (American Policy Debate)—a method of evaluating the legitimacy of an affirmative plan or negative counterplan. The predictability standard argues that if a well-researched team might have reasonably anticipated a particular plan or counterplan, then it is fair to present that plan or counterplan. For example, if the resolution requires the affirmative team to increase comprehensive health care aid to Africa, a plan that increased AIDS education would be predictable; a plan that increased veterinary care to rhinoceroses might not be.

preempt—an argument that anticipates refutation that has not yet been made. A debater who expects that his opponent might attack the constitutionality of his proposal might cite court decisions in his opening speech; a debater defending an environmental proposal might defend herself in advance against the argument that global warming is not man-made. Affirmative cases in Policy and Lincoln–Douglas debate frequently include preempts.

preference sheets—*See* strike sheets

pre-fiat implication (American Policy Debate)—reasons why the individuals participating in the debate round should adopt the negative's philosophy; in particular, why the judge's endorsement of that philosophy might lead to useful change in the debate community and beyond. For instance, the negative might present an environmental Kritik, saying that the affirmative proposal is grounded in exploitation of the natural world. The negative would ask the judge (and perhaps the participants in the round) to endorse a philosophy of harmony with nature.

preliminary round—a round of speech or debate competition in which all students at the tournament participate. Generally, one judge evaluates each preliminary round. Speakers or teams with the best performances in preliminary rounds then advance to one or more elimination rounds.

preparation time—time between speeches and/or questioning periods that teams may use to consult and plan. Each team has a strictly regulated amount of preparation time allotted to it for the entire debate. Typically, policy debate teams have 8 minutes of preparation time; Lincoln–Douglas debaters have 4; Public Forum teams have 2. Most parliamentary debate formats allow no preparation time. In Parliamentary formats, the term may refer to the time between the announcement of the topic and the starting time for the debate round.

presumption (American Policy Debate)—traditionally, the assumption that conditions and policies should remain as they are. The present system is presumed to be adequate until the affirmative team meets its burden of proving that a change in the status quo is needed or would be advantageous. Presumption is analogous to the legal principle that the accused person is presumed to be innocent until proven guilty.

prima facie case (*prima facie* is Latin for "at first look")— a case that a reasonable and prudent person would find convincing on presentation (before hearing opposing arguments). In policy debate, a prima facie case must include a specific plan to implement the resolution, proof of an inherent need for the plan, and proof that the plan would produce an advantage.

prime minister (PM) (British Parliamentary Debate, Parliamentary Debate)—the first speaker for the Government (proposition) team. The PM presents the Government's interpretation of the debate resolution, followed by major arguments in support of that resolution.

Prime Minister's Rebuttal Extension (PMRE)—an option for Government teams in Canadian Parliamentary Debate. Instead of using the standard times of 7 minutes for a constructive speech and 3 minutes for a rebuttal speech, the Government may choose to forgo 1 minute of the constructive speech and apply that minute to the rebuttal. When the PMRE is exercised, the constructive is limited to 6 minutes, the rebuttal to 4.

procedural arguments—arguments about the rules and procedures of debate, as distinct from substantive arguments about the topic area. In policy debate, the most common procedural arguments concern topicality—the question of whether the affirmative plan is, in fact, within the boundaries of the resolution. Most procedural arguments revolve around questions of fairness: whether a negative counterplan has strayed into affirmative ground or whether an affirmative plan is unacceptably vague. Procedural arguments are usually framed as absolute issues; a team that loses a procedural argument will generally lose the round regardless of the merit of their substantive arguments.

program oral interpretation (Individual Events)—a set of brief selections from two or more different genres of literature (prose, poetry, or drama) that express a theme. The program should develop the theme through the use of narrative, evocative language, and vocal characterization.

A substantial portion of the total time must be devoted to each of the genres used in the program. The use of a manuscript is required. The maximum time is 10 minutes, including an introduction. Program oral interpretation is sometimes called "mixed interpretation."

prompting—words or phrases that constitute coaching or suggestion offered by a partner during a debater's speaking time. Prompting might be a simple warning ("Go on" or "Get to the next argument!"), or it might be an additional argument or explanation. Many traditional tournament formats discourage or prohibit prompting, and some judges may penalize excessive prompting.

proposition—a debatable statement. Categories include propositions of fact ("President Obama's recent executive action on immigration violates the Constitution."), propositions of policy ("The U.S. federal government should strengthen immigration enforcement."), and propositions of value ("The United States should value the rights of citizens above the rights of noncitizens."). Proposition is synonymous with resolution or motion in some formats.

proposition (Parliamentary Debate)—the affirmative team. The Proposition team begins the debate with a case that supports the resolution. Sometimes referred to as "the Government."

proposition of fact—a debatable claim regarding objective truth. For example: "A majority of Americans favor gun control" or "The defendant committed murder in the first degree."

proposition of policy—a proposition that urges a person or group to take a particular action. "The U.S. federal government should substantially change its trade policy toward China" is an example of a proposition of policy. Policy debate topics always take this form; the word "should" is usually included.

proposition of value—a statement of belief in a concept or idea. "We ought to value liberty above equality" and "Invading another nation to prevent human rights abuses is morally justified" are propositions of value.

prosecution (Mock Trial)—students who assume the role of government attorneys who initiate and carry out a criminal action against an accused defendant.

prose interpretation (Individual Events)—an oral interpretation event in which contestants prepare a 10-minute program of excerpts from short stories, novels, or other prose literature and deliver the program from a manuscript. Prose interpretation is a standard event at college Individual Events tournaments and is sometimes offered at high school tournaments.

protected time (Parliamentary Debate)—a portion of a Parliamentary speech during which opponents' points of information may not be raised; typically, the first and last minute of the speech.

Public Forum Debate—a debate format, created by the National Forensic League in 2002, in which two-person teams argue for or against a proposition of policy or value. *See* Appendix

qualitative significance—*See* significance

quantitative significance—*See* significance

quarterfinal round—a debate elimination round consisting of eight teams, four of which would proceed to the
semifinal round. In Individual Events, quarterfinals would
include approximately 30 speakers, half of whom would
proceed to the semifinal round.

R

real world (American Policy Debate)—a topicality argument urging the judge to prefer a definition that most reasonable people would recognize as valid. Sometimes used as a response to a Kritik argument, indicating that actors in the "real world" make decisions by weighing advantages versus disadvantages rather than a consideration of philosophical implications.

reasonability (American Policy Debate)—a standard for judging whether an example or interpretation of the resolution is acceptable. Put simply, if a reasonable person would accept a case as an example of the resolution, the judge should accept it. Reasonability arguments are made by affirmative teams who are defending themselves against more technical, definition-based attacks on the topicality of their proposals.

reason for decision (RFD)—a judge's written or oral explanation of how and why she preferred one team's arguments over those of their opponents. RFDs may include explanations of the relative weight granted to competing arguments, why the judge preferred certain pieces of evidence to others, and the need for more explanation of important arguments or impacts. At tournaments that do not permit judges to discuss the round with debaters, written RFDs (read by the debaters after the tournament has concluded) are critical evaluative tools.

rebuttal—a debater's attempt to reconstruct his own arguments after an opponent has answered them. Rebuttal can be distinguished from refutation, which is an attack on an opponent's original argument. Rebuttal might be characterized as defensive argument, refutation as offensive argument.

rebuttal speech (American Policy Debate, Lincoln–Douglas Debate)—rebuttal speeches emphasize selection of arguments, comparisons of advantages and disadvantages, and, ultimately, explanations of why each team believes they have won the debate round. In policy debate, the rebuttal speeches are the third and fourth speeches given by each team, are distinct from the constructive speeches (the first and second speeches), and are 5 minutes in length. In Lincoln–Douglas, the rebuttal speeches include the first affirmative rebuttal (4 minutes), the negative rebuttal (6 minutes), and the second affirmative rebuttal (3 minutes).

rebuttal speech (Public Forum Debate)—the second speech given by each team. The first speech given by each team is a prepared case, so rebuttal speeches offer the first opportunity for each team to provide direct refutation to an opponent's argument. The team that speaks first simply answers the opposing team's case in the order of their presentation. The team that speaks second will also answer the opposing team's case and may also reserve some time to answer the opposing team's rebuttal. A rebuttal speech in Public Forum is 4 minutes.

recross (Mock Trial)—resumption of questioning by the original cross-examiner. Recross follows redirect; it responds to points or information that may have surfaced during cross-examination.

red herring—an irrelevant argument or observation that misleads or detracts from substantive discussion. For example, if the affirmative argues "We need to expand city bus service" and the negative counters "The buses are frequently dirty. Why can't we keep the buses clean?" the negative has introduced a red herring.

redirect (Mock Trial)—resumption of questioning by the original examiner. Redirect follows cross-examination; it responds to points or information that may have surfaced during recross.

referendum counterplan (American Policy Debate)— a negative proposal that submits the affirmative plan to a popular vote. Negative teams presenting this counterplan will argue that it gains the affirmative's advantages, plus the additional advantage of increased participatory democracy. Some teams will also argue that government policies work better if citizens are consulted about their implementation and are invested in the outcome of the policy. Affirmative teams might respond by highlighting the risk that voters would not approve the proposal and by arguing that the negative has illegitimately shifted debate from the merits of the proposal to its means of implementation. Some affirmative teams might also argue that participatory democracy is not always advantageous.

refutation—the process of attacking and destroying opposing arguments (as distinguished from advancing or defending one's own arguments).

reply speech (Parliamentary Debate)—an optional feature in Australia-Asia Debate. If rules permit, either the first or second speaker on a team may make a reply speech, with the negative (Opposition) team speaking first.

reply speech (World Schools Debate)—the closing speech for each side in the World Schools Debate format. Each reply speaker will offer a final refutation of opposing argument, advance her or his own arguments, and provide a summary of the round.

resolution (American Policy, Lincoln–Douglas, and Public Forum debates)—a formal expression of intention or opinion presented in the form of a motion for purposes of debate. For example, Resolved: That the U.S. federal government should reduce aid to Pakistan.

resolutional focus (American Policy Debate)—the belief that debate should focus on the resolution as a general statement rather than on examples or subsets of the resolution. If the topic called for the U.S. federal government to increase space exploration, resolutional focus would dictate that the debaters discuss a general increase, including several types of space exploration, rather than one specific program. This is distinct from plan focus, which emphasizes debate about a specific example of the resolution.

resolved clause (Congressional Debate)—language at the end of a resolution that expresses the opinion or judgment of the House ("Be it resolved: that this House supports continued economic sanctions against Iran.").

reverse voting issue (RVI) (Lincoln–Douglas Debate)—a type of affirmative answer to a negative topicality (or other theory) argument. Reverse voting issues claim that if the negative can win the round absolutely on a single topicality argument, then they should also risk losing the round absolutely if they lose that argument. Some RVI arguments also claim that the negative's theory arguments are essentially frivolous distractions from substantive argument and that such tactics should be punished. RVI arguments were first developed in policy debate, but are now heard much more often in Lincoln–Douglas Debate.

reversibility (American Policy Debate)—a standard for evaluating competing impacts. Assume a debate in which the affirmative claims that, without their plan, the American standard of living will decline; and the negative argues that the affirmative plan will hasten global warming. The negative might argue that their impact is more important because economic decline is reversible, but climate change is not.

RFD–*See* reason for decision

rhetoric—the art of written and spoken discourse, particularly discourse that aims to inform, persuade, or motivate an audience. According to Aristotle, rhetoric comprises "the available means of persuasion," including ethos (the credibility of the speaker), pathos (appeals to the emotions), and logos (appeals through rational argument).

rhetorical categories—*See* ethos, logos, pathos

rhetorical criticism (Individual Events)—an original speech by the student designed to offer an explanation and/or evaluation of a communication event such as a speech, speaker, movement, poem, poster, film, campaign, etc., through the use of rhetorical principles. Audio-visual aids may or may not be used to supplement and reinforce the message. Manuscripts are permitted. Maximum time is 10 minutes. Rhetorical criticism is offered at college Individual Events tournaments sponsored by the National Forensic Association; it is similar to communication analysis, offered at tournaments sponsored by the American Forensic Association.

rhetorical situation—a concept made popular by the rhetorical scholar Lloyd Bitzer; it describes the context that surrounds a speech act, including the considerations (e.g., purpose, audience, author/speaker, and constraints) that play a role in how the act is produced and perceived by its audience.

rising vote—*See* floor vote

roadmap—a brief introductory statement that presents the organizational pattern a debater intends to follow in her speech. ("I'm going to begin with topicality, then the counterplan, and then go back to arguments on their second advantage. Is everyone ready?").

role of the ballot—the meaning and purpose of the judge's decision within the context of the debate, increasingly discussed as an issue within the round. One team might argue that the role of the ballot is to reward the best-crafted arguments, while an opposing team might argue that the judge has a duty to endorse a particular political goal or encourage a particular type of argument.

role playing—the assumption that academic tournament debate imitates other settings and that debaters should behave like actors in those settings. Parliamentary and policy debate assume, in different ways, that the speakers are members of a legislative body. Most forms of debate are role playing in that students often advocate arguments with which they may not agree. Role playing is being increasingly challenged by coaches and debaters who see debate as a vehicle for authentic advocacy in which students present only arguments that they themselves believe.

round—a debate contest in which speeches of specified length follow one another in a specified order. Tournaments consist of as few as three and as many as eight preliminary rounds, followed by a designated number of elimination rounds for the best-performing debaters.

RVI—*See* reverse voting issue

s

sandbagging—a tactic that initially disguises a strong argument as a weak argument that is then argued in full force in a later speech. Most commonly, a negative team employs sandbagging to catch an affirmative team off guard.

scenario—a step-by-step explanation of how a proposal might result in, or prevent, a catastrophic impact. ("Our plan has the U.S. government sell arms to Pakistan. This reassures the Pakistani government of our support and will restrain Chinese aggressive tendencies in South Asia, thus reducing the chance of regional war.") Affirmative teams may present scenarios as explanations of their advantages; negative teams will present them in disadvantages to affirmative proposals. Many affirmative cases and negative disadvantages contain multiple scenarios, each with chains of causality supported by evidence.

schematic—a chart displayed or distributed at tournaments that details the pairings, judge assignments, and locations of a particular round.

second affirmative (American Policy Debate)—the second speaker on the affirmative team. The second affirmative constructive reestablishes the affirmative case and answers attacks made by the first negative constructive. The second affirmative rebuttal is the last speech in a policy debate; it attempts a synthesis of all the key arguments in the debate, with the goal of proving that the advantages of the affirmative proposal outweigh any disadvantages and are superior to any alternatives.

second negative (American Policy Debate)—the second speaker on the negative team. The second negative constructive advances some of the issues presented in the first negative constructive (leaving others for his partner to discuss in the first negative rebuttal). The second negative rebuttal narrows the debate to one or two key issues and attempts to persuade the judge to vote on those issues.

secret topic debates (Parliamentary Debate)—a form of Asian Parliamentary Debate in which sides and topics are revealed only an hour prior to the debate. This contrasts with the usual Asians practice of revealing the topic one or more days before the tournament.

seeding—the ranking of teams prior to elimination rounds. A team's win-loss record, followed by its speaker points, determines its seeding.

semifinal round—a debate elimination round consisting of four teams, two of which will proceed to the final round. In Individual Events, a semifinal round would include 12–15 students, approximately half of whom would advance to the final round.

severance (American Policy Debate)—an instance in which a team claims the right to abandon parts of its plan or counterplan text during the round. Generally, opposing teams will argue that severance represents an unfair shift in advocacy.

severance permutation (American Policy Debate)—a permutation that tests a counterplan by arguing that part of the plan (but not the entire plan) competes with the counterplan. Assume an affirmative plan in which the U.S. federal government establishes and funds a road and bridge repair program; the negative counterplans with 50-state action. The affirmative argues a permutation in which the states fund a federally administered program, thereby severing the funding portion of their original plan. Many judges regard severance permutations as an unfair shift in advocacy.

shift—a significant change in advocacy during the round. Shifts might include a change in the affirmative plan text or an entirely new interpretation of a key negative argument. Most judges regard shifts as illegitimate.

short diagonal (British Parliamentary Debate)—the interaction between the Opening Opposition and Closing Government speakers.

short preparation debates (Asian Parliamentary Debate)—a contest for which the resolution is announced less than a day in advance. This is in contrast to most topics in this format, which are announced days or weeks in advance. Short preparation debates may also place restrictions on the materials that teams may consult as they prepare.

should—an important term in many debate topics; usually defined as "ought to, but not necessarily will." This term is always used in propositions of policy. Affirmative cases justify a proposal by showing that it will produce an advantage and *should* be adopted, regardless of whether the relevant government body *would* adopt the proposal at the present time.

significance—the degree of importance of a conclusion. Significance may be qualitative or quantitative. Qualitative significance rests on an established value; quantitative significance rests on concrete units of measurement. Traditional judges regard significance as a stock issue and believe that affirmative teams must prove not merely a harmful condition in the present system; but a harm that might be considered significant.

signposting—ongoing verbal communication of an organizational pattern. Good signposting is crucial to organization in any "flow" debate round. Essentially, signposting involves consistent, concise references to the specific argument being answered (by number or by label) and to one's own arguments, as well as clear transition language indicating that the speaker is moving to a different issue. ("Let's go to the first advantage now. My opponent's first argument says that global warming is not man-made, but I have two answers. First, I'd refer you to the McKibben evidence, which summarizes several good studies. Second, even if it isn't man-made, we still need to try to reverse its effects. Now let's look at the second advantage.")

sign reasoning—cause-and-effect reasoning from example; an assertion that two or more things are so closely related that one causes the other ("Where there is fire, there is smoke."; "Anne wears a gold band on the third finger of her left hand; she must be married.").

skills judging—a style of judging in which a judge emphasizes organization, rhetoric, and speaking skills rather than the resolution of substantive arguments. Some skills judges are lay judges; others may have academic backgrounds in speech communication but not in formal argumentation.

snug case (Parliamentary Debate)—a case that is considered difficult, but not impossible, to debate. Typically a snug case leaves little ground for counterargument ("This House would improve aviation security."). Although valid objections might be raised to specific security methods, no one would oppose the goal of making airplanes safer. Opposition teams will usually object to snug cases and attempt to convince the judge that they are illegitimate.

solvency (American Policy Debate)—the relationship of workability between a policy and its claimed effects. Solvency is a policy debate stock issue and is a key focus of most policy debates; if an affirmative cannot prove that they solve the problem they have identified, they will lose the round. For instance, an affirmative plan might claim to reduce death and injury through a program of road and bridge repair; if they succeed to some degree, solvency has occurred. A negative team might argue that a lack of sufficient funding, engineering difficulties, or bureaucratic obstacles will ultimately prevent any advantage from occurring, therefore, they claim that the affirmative has no solvency.

solvency advocate (American Policy Debate)—an expert whose published work promotes a policy option similar to the affirmative plan. Identifying an advocate is a key feature of affirmative solvency.

spar debates—very brief debate rounds, often used to introduce beginners to competition or as practice exercises for more experienced debaters. Speech times vary, but usually no speech is longer than 90 seconds. Spar debates often discuss very narrow topics or subsets of a larger debate topic. Spar debate is occasionally offered as a distinct competitive event.

speaker points—a numerical score assigned to each debater by the judge. Most tournaments use a 30-point system, with 30 as maximum; half points and other fractions are increasingly permitted. Assigning speaker points is independent of the judge's win-loss decision; on occasion, winning teams may receive fewer speaker points than losing teams. Speaker points, together with win-loss records, are used to determine the seeding of teams as the tournament proceeds and determine placement in the elimination bracket. Additionally, individual speaker awards are based on points.

speaking order (Individual Events)—the sequence in which Individual Events competitors perform. Tournament pairings will prescribe speaking order for each section of each event. Unless a student is entered in two events which are scheduled in the same time bracket, she will be expected to speak in the order listed on the schematic. Since contestants who speak first or last are generally believed to have a competitive advantage, tournaments try to ensure that speaking order for each student varies from round to round.

spec case—specialized knowledge case

specialized knowledge case (Parliamentary Debate)—A case that is only debatable if the opposition has specialized knowledge. A government case requiring winemakers to reduce their use of cultured yeast, for instance, would be impossible to answer intelligently without a detailed grasp of oenology. Few judges will tolerate specialized knowledge cases, and opposition teams will generally object to cases that violate the "general knowledge" standard. Also known as specific-knowledge case.

specific-knowledge case—*See* specialized knowledge case

speed ballot—a detachable piece of a ballot that includes spaces for decision and speaker points. This can be returned to the tabulation room quickly; the judge then has more time to write comments on the main part of the ballot.

speed reading—*See* spreading

spending disadvantage (American Policy Debate)—a generic negative argument asserting that new spending required by the affirmative plan will harm the economy. Spending disadvantages generally assume a current economic condition in which federal government spending has reached an upper limit of sustainability; new federal government spending required by the plan would discomfit investors, cause an undesirable level of inflation, or enrage members of Congress (who might retaliate by sabotaging other desirable programs). The negative may argue that the impact of new spending will be recession or depression, with the latter impact possibly increasing the risk of war. Affirmative teams might argue, in response, that their proposal will actually not cause new spending, that additional spending now would not disturb the economy, or that the benefits of new spending would outweigh the harms.

spike (American Policy Debate)—language intended to preempt an opposing argument. In policy debate, an affirmative team, fearing arguments against deficit spending, might specify that their plan will be funded by diverting money from other government programs. In Lincoln–Douglas, a debater might begin her presentation by arguing that certain types of ethical argument are illegitimate.

sponsorship speech—*See* authorship speech

spreading—speaking well above conversational speed; attempting to maximize the number of arguments made in the allotted time, sometimes at the expense of clarity or completeness. Spreading is most often practiced in policy debate, though it is increasingly found in Lincoln–Douglas rounds; it is strongly discouraged in other formats.

squirrel (n.)—an elimination round judge who votes in the minority, for example, "Jane was the squirrel in the quarterfinal round."

squirrel (v.) (Parliamentary Debate)—to derive a resolution or case from a vague topic. For instance, a Parliamentary tournament might offer a topic consisting simply of the words "Lady Gaga." An affirmative or Government team might then interpret the topic as "Lady Gaga concerts should be banned," and present reasons why this is true.

squirrel case—an unusual or counterintuitive affirmative case designed to surprise an opponent. Squirrel cases usually are based on an unusual interpretation of the resolution, address an extremely small subset of the resolution, or (in some Parliamentary formats) present a resolution that the negative finds very difficult or impossible to contest.

squo—*See* status quo

statement of facts (Mock Trial)—a narrative account of the events and information relevant to the legal proceeding. Put simply, a statement of facts recounts what happened, where, and when. A statement of facts does not make an argument; rather, it summarizes the verifiable, objective information that both the prosecution and the defense have agreed on. A statement of facts is included in the case packet that is presented to both sides several weeks prior to the competition.

status quo (American Policy Debate)—the present system; the existing order; that which would be changed by adopting the affirmative plan. Defense of the status quo is usually the core of any negative strategy, although counterplans and Kritik arguments may also advocate a change in the present system. Sometimes abbreviated as the "squo."

stipulation (Mock Trial)—issues that both sides have agreed to prior to the trial. For instance, both parties may have agreed on the authenticity of the exhibits and affidavits, the competence of the expert witnesses, and the good conduct of the investigating officers. Stipulations serve to place such issues off-limits, or outside the realm of discussion, during the Mock Trial proceeding. A list of stipulations is included in the case packet that is presented to both sides several weeks prior to the competition.

Stoa USA—a forensics organization dedicated to supporting Christian students in the United States who are homeschooled. Stoa is named after the portico that marked a site of public debate in towns in ancient Greece. Stoa helps to support and coordinate state and local homeschool tournaments, leagues, and clubs; additionally, it sponsors the National Invitational Tournament of Champions.

stock issues (American Policy Debate)—a series of broad questions encompassing the major debatable issues of any proposition of policy. Most theorists include significance, harm, inherency, solvency, and topicality as stock issues. The affirmative must prove all stock issues to win the round.

straight link (Parliamentary Debate)—a type of Parliamentary topic that leaves no room for reinterpretation or refinement by the Government team. "The United States should assassinate President Bashar al-Assad" would be an example of a straight link.

straight refutation—argument as contradiction. For every claim the affirmative asserts is true, the negative offers a counterclaim asserting that what the affirmative says is false.

straight turn (American Policy Debate)—a strategic affirmative response to a negative disadvantage in which the affirmative argues only that the disadvantage is, in fact, an advantage.

straw man—a fallacy in which a debater deliberately misrepresents an argument and then answers the misrepresentation rather than the argument that has actually been presented. (Affirmative: "We should legalize marijuana for medical uses." Negative: "My opponent advocates the complete decriminalization of marijuana! This would be harmful to society for five reasons . . . ").

strike—a veto exercised by a school or team against a judge. Tournaments that permit strikes typically present schools with a list of the judges in attendance and allow a limited number of strikes; judges who are struck will not be assigned to hear that school's debaters. No reasons for strikes need be given. Typically, teams strike judges if a) they think the judge is incompetent; b) they think the judge is completely unwilling to give their arguments or types of arguments a fair hearing; c) prior experience has convinced them that the judge is prejudiced against them.

strike sheets—a list of tournament judges provided in advance of competition. Contestants and coaches may then veto a limited number of judges whom they do not prefer.

structural inherency (American Policy Debate)—a law or structure in the status quo that prevents a solution to a problem. As an example, consider a case that attempts to improve the economic standing of immigrants. Many immigrants cannot take jobs that require them to drive or are in locations not served by public transportation. Forty states still deny drivers' licenses to noncitizens; this is a legal structure that keeps that harm in place.

study counterplan (American Policy Debate)—a negative proposal that subjects the affirmative plan to further study by government agencies or other experts. The plan then becomes law only after recommended revisions are incorporated.

summary speech (Public Forum Debate)—the next-to-last speech given by each team. Summary speeches are 2 minutes long. They follow the rebuttal speeches and precede the final focus speeches. Typically, summary speakers reduce the number of arguments discussed and work to identify the key issues in the debate.

swing team—a team added to a tournament field at the last moment to create an even number of contestants and avoid the awarding of byes. Often the swing team is supplied by the host school.

switch side—debating both affirmative and negative sides of a resolution, usually in alternate rounds.

syllogism—a form of deductive reasoning in which a necessary conclusion is drawn from two premises (major and minor). ("All cows are mammals. Daisy is a cow. Therefore, Daisy is a mammal.")

T

tag (American Policy Debate)—a one sentence statement that summarizes the thesis of a quotation used in evidence and states its significance in the debate.

takeout (American Policy Debate)—direct, absolute refutation contradicting an opposing argument. If the negative argues that the affirmative plan will require additional government revenue, an affirmative claim that no new spending will be required functions as a takeout. A takeout nullifies an opposing argument, as opposed to a turnaround, which converts a supposed disadvantage into an advantage.

tautologies—arguments that repeat the same thought but use different words. For example, "Good citizens should help the poor"—with "goodness" defined as "a willingness to do charitable acts"—is a circular resolution; the negative has no ground here.

team split (Parliamentary Debate)—in Australia-Asia Debate, the division of labor between the first two speakers. The first speaker communicates the team split to the judge.

Ted Turner Debate (Public Forum Debate)—the original name for Public Forum Debate, developed by the National Forensic League (now the National Speech and Debate Association) and named after the CNN founder and American media executive Ted Turner.

textual competition (American Policy Debate)—textual competition occurs when the counterplan (or alternative) text competes because its wording conflicts with the wording of the affirmative plan. This is distinct from functional competition, in which the counterplan's essential action competes with the affirmative's. For instance, a counterplan that substitutes the word "humankind" for the affirmative's "mankind" would be textually competitive but not functionally competitive.

theory arguments—claims about the nature of the debate process itself, as distinct from claims about the substance of the topic under discussion. Topicality, the most widely used theory argument, addresses not only whether the affirmative is actually defending the resolution as worded, but why it is important that they do so. Other theory arguments concern the distinction between affirmative and negative ground, what burdens a negative counterplan must meet, and whether discussion of policy should be preferred to discussion of ethics or philosophy. Theory arguments are very common in policy debate, they are increasingly found in Lincoln–Douglas and are occasionally employed in Public Forum and some Parliamentary events.

tight case (American Parliamentary Debate)—a case phrased or constructed to avoid any reasonable opposing argument. "This House would improve bicycle safety," for instance, leaves very little opposition ground; everyone favors safety. The opposition will usually argue that such a case is illegitimate and should be voted down.

tight link (American Parliamentary Debate)—a type of Parliamentary case in which the topic directs the debaters to specific subject matter, but allows the Government some leeway in interpreting the topic. "This House would adopt a new strategy in the War on Terror" restricts the debate to a discussion of terrorism, but permits the Government to decide what the "new strategy" might be.

time frame—a classic component of decision calculus. A debater may argue that his impact is more important than his opponent's because his will occur sooner. ("The affirmative claims to prevent environmental collapse at some indefinite point in the future. But we prove that their plan will trigger a recession within a year and could cause a devastating world depression within three years. Prefer our impacts because of this time frame.")

time frame permutation (American Policy Debate)—a test of counterplan competition that argues that the plan and counterplan need not be done simultaneously and that doing one before the other could achieve the net benefits that the counterplan claims.

time limits—rules regarding the duration of speeches (or preparation time) in a speech or debate event.

time-space case (Parliamentary Debate)—a type of Parliamentary Debate case that assumes a specific historical context and argues for a specific course of action that should have been taken. "President Harry Truman should not have used atomic weapons against Japan" is an example of a time-space case.

time suck (American Policy Debate)—an argument presented primarily to waste an opponent's limited time.

topicality (American Policy Debate)—one of the standard points of controversy, or stock issues, in policy debate.

An affirmative plan is topical if it meets the terms of the debate resolution; topicality arguments address that question. If the resolution requires the affirmative team to "reduce air and water pollution," and the plan addresses only air pollution, the negative might argue that the affirmative is not topical—they have not done what the resolution tells them they must do.

topic selection—the process of selecting a debate resolution. High school policy debate topic selection is governed by the National Federation of State High School Activities Associations, which issues a call for topic proposals. A national topic selection meeting, held each August, selects topic options from among those papers. States vote on those topic options the following January, thus the topic for the coming school year is available eight months in advance. Lincoln–Douglas and Public Forum topic selection is governed by the National Forensic League, which puts topic choices to a vote of its member schools, with topics announced a month in advance of their implementation. College policy topic selection is governed by the Cross Examination Debate Association; its member institutions vote on the list of topics it provides.

Toulmin model—a model of argument developed by the philosopher Stephen Toulmin and presented in his 1958 book, *The Uses of Argument.* Toulmin identifies the essential components of argument as the claim (a conclusion or thesis); the data (facts that support the claim); and the warrant (the connection between the data and the claim). An example would be:

> *Claim*: I am qualified to teach high school chemistry.

Data: I have a chemistry teaching certificate.

Warrant: Persons who have a chemistry teaching certificate are qualified to teach chemistry.

Toulmin also stipulates that strong arguments might include backing (additional warrants supporting the main warrant), rebuttal (answers to probable counterarguments), and qualifiers (which express degrees of certainty or acknowledge exceptions to the general statement).

tournament—a competitive setting in which students practice their arguments and sharpen their thinking and speaking skills. Tournaments consist of a fixed number of preliminary rounds in which all students compete, followed by elimination rounds for teams with the best preliminary records. Many tournaments offer intermediate (sometimes called "junior varsity") and novice divisions, in addition to open divisions (generally directed at the most experienced debaters). Awards are presented to most teams who reach elimination rounds and to individual speakers with the highest point totals. *See* junior varsity, open division

trade-off disadvantage (American Policy Debate)—a negative argument claiming that funding of the affirmative plan would result in a reduction in funding for some other, more desirable, government program. For instance, an affirmative team might propose an expansion in science education; the negative might argue that there is a limit to the amount of money that the government can spend on education and that increases in science education funding might require reductions in early-childhood education.

transitional movement—physical movement that indicates or reinforces a transition from one main idea to another; most often occurring in Individual Events, especially extemporaneous speaking.

triathlon (Individual Events)—a special award category for speakers who enter three or more events at one tournament. Generally, triathlon awards are based on performance in one event from each major category of Individual Events: limited preparation, platform, and interpretive events.

triple octafinal round—an elimination round consisting of 64 teams, 32 of which will advance to a double octafinal round; found only in very large tournaments.

truism—an argument that is not disputable. "Barack Obama was the greatest Democratic president of the United States since Bill Clinton" is not debatable; there have been no other Democratic presidents since Bill Clinton.

tu quoque (Latin for "and you also")—an ad hominem argument that notes inconsistency between a person's conduct or beliefs and the argument he makes. A candidate for office might argue for stricter control of immigration; her opponent might note that the candidate herself has employed illegal immigrants. A debater might advocate ethical treatment of animals; an opponent might call attention to his leather shoes or fur jacket. Tu quoque appeals may succeed in reducing a debater's credibility even as they fail to engage the merits of her argument directly.

turnaround—a response that makes an opponent's argument support the speaker's position.

U

unconditional argument—an argument or proposal that a team will advocate throughout the round regardless of how it is answered by opponents.

underview—a brief synthesis of the issues under discussion, usually offered at the end of a rebuttal speech. An underview contrasts with line-by-line discussion in which each particular argument is answered systematically and in order.

uniqueness (American Policy Debate)—the condition of intrinsic or necessary connection between a policy and a result. If an advantage or disadvantage would happen if a plan were implemented, but not otherwise, that advantage or disadvantage is unique. Uniqueness is a crucial burden of any disadvantage argued by the negative. For instance, a negative team refuting an affirmative plan that places economic sanctions on Venezuela might argue that the affirmative plan would result in increased oil prices; that disadvantage is unique if they can also prove that oil prices would not rise absent the plan.

United Asian Debating Championships (UADC) (Parliamentary Debate)—an annual debating tournament held each May for university debate teams throughout Asia. It is the largest intervarsity Parliamentary Debate tournament in Asia, with more than 600 participants. The competition involves eight preliminary rounds, followed by a break to octafinals. A separate elimination round bracket is announced for English as Foreign Language team competition.

urban debate leagues (UDL) (American Policy Debate)—Urban debate leagues provide competitive debate opportunities to inner-city youth throughout the United States. They work predominantly with minority students and focus exclusively on policy debate. The UDL concept began with debate initiatives in the early 1980s in Detroit and Atlanta—cities whose public school systems lacked the funding and expertise to sponsor debate teams without assistance. The Detroit Public Debate League began in 1984 as an after-school partnership between the Detroit Gifted and Talented Program and Wayne State University director of debate George Ziegemueller. The initial Atlanta UDL was formed as a partnership between Emory University's Barkley Forum, under the direction of Melissa Maxcy Wade, and the Atlanta Public Schools.

Early program support for urban debate initiatives came from the National Forensic League and the Phillips Petroleum Company. George Soros's Open Society Institute (OSI [now Open Society Foundations]) became involved in 1997, providing seed money to establish leagues throughout the country based on the Atlanta model. By 2000, OSI had provided seed and support funding for leagues in Baltimore, Chicago, Kansas City, New York, Providence, St. Louis, Tuscaloosa, the San Francisco Bay area, and Southern California; other leagues formed in Boston, Dallas, Houston, Los Angeles, Newark, Miami, Milwaukee, Minneapolis-St. Paul, Seattle, and Washington D.C.

In 2002, the National Association for Urban Debate Leagues was created to provide national leadership for local leagues—in large part by assisting leagues with the development of their own fund-raising operations to replace the OSI seed money. Today, urban debate leagues are funded primarily by one of three local institutions: urban public school systems, nonprofit organizations dedicated to establishing a local UDL, or university debate programs engaged in community outreach. Most urban debate leagues recruit and train urban educators as coaches, though many also use university debaters or former debaters within the community to serve as assistant coaches. While all UDLs attempt to recruit volunteer support (e.g., tournament judges, tournament tab room coordinators, and lecturers at debate workshops for students), certain core costs of a UDL, including coach stipends, debate materials, and transportation to tournaments, must be funded for a program to be sustainable.

Urban debate has expanded to include debate across the curriculum (as a classroom learning tool), public debates (partnering with community-based organizations), debates in prisons, and middle school competitions. The National Association of Urban Debate Leagues (NAUDL), local leagues, and university programs affiliated with UDLs have sponsored significant research supporting the social and educational value of urban competitive debate. The NAUDL national tournament, established in 2008, brings the strongest urban debaters together each spring for a weekend of competition and education. By 2010, more than 40,000 urban public school students from 400 different high schools had competed in UDL tournaments.

V

value—an underlying belief or assumption, moral or ethical, with wide enough acceptance to validate conclusions that are derived from it. Some debates, especially in Lincoln–Douglas, are devoted entirely to propositions of value ("Resolved: That liberty is more important than equality."). But values also underlie decisions about which policies should be adopted. For instance, a debate about reform of the criminal justice system will quickly engage questions of the ethics of capital punishment or whether we should value individual freedom above safety.

value criterion (Lincoln–Douglas Debate)—a standard for determining which debater best defends a philosophical principle. For instance, one debater defending the value of justice might declare that the best way to determine whether justice is achieved is to examine whether defendants receive due process of law. Another debater might argue that justice is best measured by its success in removing criminals from society. Each debater would attempt to persuade the judge that his vision of justice is superior.

value premise (Lincoln–Douglas Debate)—a philosophical principle that underlies and unifies a debater's arguments. A value premise might consist of a classic philosophical viewpoint (utilitarianism or deontology), or it might be a more common political concept (liberty or justice). Where the two debaters' values coincide, each may attempt to show how their case better advances the commonly held value. If the values are in conflict, the debaters' goal will be to explain which value society should prefer.

vocalized pause—a "filler" word or phrase (e.g., "um," "er," "you know") supplied by the brain as it searches mentally for the next word or idea. Debaters and extemporaneous speakers work hard to eliminate vocalized pauses from their speeches.

voting issue—an argument claimed to govern a judge's decision. Debaters often describe the policy debate stock issues—topicality and solvency, for instance—as voting issues, as are arguments with large impacts such as disadvantages. ("Our disadvantage proves that the problems caused by global warming outweigh any advantage of economic growth; this is a *voting issue*.")

walkover—two teams from the same school meeting in a tournament elimination round. ("Northwestern had a walkover in one of the semifinal rounds." "Susie and Brent got walked over by Bill and Brad.") If a walkover happens in a round before finals, a coach must choose which team will advance to the next elimination rounds. A walkover is sometimes called a "closeout."

warm ups—vocal exercises performed before rounds to sharpen enunciation and vocal quality. Warm ups may include tongue twisters, singing, and enunciation drills. Warm ups are sometimes a team ritual, with an entire squad vocalizing together before the first round of a tournament.

warrant—the reason why a claim is true. For instance, a debater might argue that investment in road and bridge repair and expansion would improve the economy. Her first warrant might be that building roads would create new jobs; another warrant might be that better roads mean more efficient transportation of goods.

weighing—a comparison of impacts made by a debater. Generally, both sides in a debate will argue that a course of action will produce certain advantages or disadvantages. In late speeches, debaters often compare the advantages and disadvantages using criteria such as the magnitude of the impact, its certainty, the risk, and the time frame of the impact. An affirmative debater, for instance, might argue that his proposal to expand manufacturing will prevent a short-term economic crisis and that this advantage outweighs a small additional risk of long-term damage to the environment.

whereas clause (Congressional Debate)—prefatory language in a resolution that presents findings or information that contextualizes the resolution ("Whereas the Iranian government has routinely ignored diplomatic overtures . . . "). A resolution may include several whereas clauses.

whip—*See* Government whip, Opposition whip

white copy—a half-sheet of paper containing only the judge's decision and speaker points (with complete comments to be written later on the actual ballot). Sometimes known as a "speed ballot."

whole resolution (whole res) (American Policy Debate)—a generic debate argument that says that the resolution must be debated holistically to determine its probable truth. For example, an affirmative team defending a resolution on comprehensive prison reform might present a specific plan to reduce prison overcrowding; the negative would argue that the affirmative must defend the entire scope of prison reform, not merely one facet or example of reform.

wing (World Schools Debate)—an adjudicator on a panel who is not the chair.

word economy—the omission of needless words. Time constraints in competitive events make word economy vital to success in debate, extemporaneous, and impromptu speaking.

word PIC (American Policy Debate)—a counterplan that adopts the essential action of the affirmative plan but alters the language of its text, usually by the substitution of one word. A word PIC frequently claims that the discourse of the affirmative proposal is unacceptable and must be rejected. For instance, an affirmative proposal that addresses the problems of handicapped persons might be opposed by a counterplan that replaces the word "handicapped" with the phrase "differently abled."

workability (American Policy Debate)—a condition whereby a proposal could actually operate to solve a problem if implemented as legislation. Negative teams might argue that an affirmative plan ought not be adopted because it is not workable—for instance, a plan to increase medical care in Africa might be unworkable because not enough doctors will be willing to work in Africa.

World Individual Debating and Public Speaking Championships (WIDPSC)—an annual international English-language debating and public speaking tournament for individual high school–level students representing different countries. It is held during a five-day period in late March and involves 180–200 competitors.

The tournament was founded in 1988 by a number of British and American secondary schools, partly to respond to the desire for an equivalent competition for public speaking at the international level. The tournament usually takes five days, with two to three rounds of events daily.

The tournament offers four events: Parliamentary Debate (using a World Schools format); impromptu speaking; interpretive reading (prose, poetry, dramatic literature, or some combination); and either persuasive speaking or after-dinner speaking. Students compete in two preliminary rounds of each event. The judging pool is comprised largely of members of the general public who have participated in one or more judge-training workshops. A competitor will be judged by 40 to 50 judges in the course of the competition.

The top 7 to 12 competitors in each event advance to final rounds (actually, semifinal rounds), with the top 2 competitors or teams in the final rounds advancing to the grand finals. The grand finals are judged by invited guests—often media personalities, political officials, or other prominent individuals.

Although most WIDPSC contestants are from English-speaking countries, the competition has increasingly attracted much broader participation, including students from Argentina, Botswana, Cyprus, Germany, Israel, Lithuania, Pakistan, South Korea, and Zimbabwe. Competitors can qualify through direct application via their national forensics organization or through special national qualifying tournaments.

World Schools Debate—a "purpose built" format that asks speakers to grapple with general issues rather than specific programs or proposals. *See* Appendix

World Schools Debating Championships (WSDC)—an annual English-language debating tournament for high school–level teams representing different countries. The competition has grown rapidly since its inception in 1988;

in recent years, more than 40 nations have been represented. Although the tournament is conducted in English, many teams represent non-English-speaking countries, and special English as a second language and English as a foreign language elimination rounds are held in addition to open division elimination rounds.

World Schools Debating Championship debates use a special format known as "World Schools Style Debating." This is a combination of the British Parliamentary and Australian formats, in which each debate comprises eight speeches delivered by two three-member teams (the Proposition and the Opposition). Each speaker delivers an 8-minute speech; then both teams deliver a "reply speech" lasting 4 minutes, with the last word being reserved for the Proposition.

The WSDC is normally held over the course of 10 days. Each national team competes in eight preliminary debates: four prepared debates (the motion having been announced a few weeks before the start of the tournament), and four impromptu debates (for which teams have 1 hour to prepare). Once the eight preliminary rounds have been completed, the 16 best teams compete in elimination brackets.

The World Schools Debating Championships is governed by the World Schools Debating Council, made up of representatives of each of the countries that participate in the championships.

Worlds Format Debate (Worlds)—a hybrid of different Parliamentary Debate styles. Like all Parliamentary Debate formats, Worlds emphasizes argument before a general audience; logic and rhetoric are more important than extensive research or debate technicalities. Topics (known in Worlds as "motions") are announced either 15 minutes before the debate or at the very beginning of the debate. Debaters argue from their own broad knowledge; actual quotation of evidence is prohibited. Worlds varies by country and tournament but has two main formats: World Schools Debate, for secondary school students, and Worlds University Debate, for university students.

Worlds University Debate—Worlds Format Debate for college and university students. It is very similar to British Parliamentary debate and distinct from World Schools Debate, which is for secondary schools.

World Universities Debating Championship (WUDC)—founded in 1981, it was the first major international debate competition for university students and is one of the largest. Each year, the event is hosted by a university selected by the World Universities Debating Council. The tournament is colloquially referred to as "Worlds." In recent years, 150–400 teams have competed over a period of six days. Although the majority of teams are from English-speaking countries, in recent years teams from Asian and African nations have increased their participation. The tournament is usually held in late December and early January; teams debate in nine preliminary rounds and as many as five elimination rounds.

The contest format is very similar to British Parliamentary Debate, although teams of two (rather than three) compete. Four teams compete in each round, two for the Government and two for the Opposition. (This differs from the World Schools [secondary school] format, which uses teams of three and which refers to the team upholding the resolution as the "Proposition," rather than the "Opposition.")

The Worlds tournament maintains separate elimination brackets for the English-as-a-second language and English-as-a-foreign language team competitions, for the individual public speaking competition, and for the "World Masters" tournament, which has judges (most of whom are no longer students) as debaters representing the countries where they studied or of which they are citizens.

The tournament is administered by the World Universities Debating Council, which consists of representatives of every country that competes at the World Universities Debating Championship. The council is responsible for setting the rules and awarding the right to host the championships.

WUDC—*See* World Universities Debating Championship

APPENDIX: MAJOR DEBATE FORMATS

AMERICAN POLICY DEBATE

Overview

American Policy Debate, sometimes called "team debate" (to distinguish it from Lincoln–Douglas Debate) or "cross-examination debate" (sometimes shortened to Cross-X, CX, Cross-ex, or C-X), focuses on a proposition of policy—what course of action the U.S. federal government should take regarding a current public issue. Two-person teams, prepared to debate either the affirmative or negative side in any given round, compete in this format. Policy debate is generally regarded as the most research-intensive style of debate, and the arguments are often complex. Because there is just one topic for the academic year and because the topic (especially the high school topic) is established far in advance of any tournament competition, students are able to and do delve deeply into all aspects of the resolution. Policy debate is also the least "audience-friendly" form of debate, as debaters assume (usually correctly) that their judges are experienced critics with a significant knowledge base. As policy has become more technical and specialized, and as more accessible debate events have become popular, the number of high schools and universities fielding policy teams has declined, although the level of participation has stabilized in recent years.

History

Interscholastic policy debate had its origins in nineteenth-century collegiate debating societies in which students would engage in (often public) debates against their classmates. Throughout the nineteenth and early twentieth centuries, debate topics were, variously, propositions of policy or value; debate formats were not standardized. American high school policy debate began to develop as a distinct activity in 1925 with the formation of the National Forensic League. College policy debate became codified in 1947 with the establishment of the National Debate Tournament. By this time, both high school and college policy debate had established nationwide conventions: two-person teams, eight speeches (four for each side), and year-long policy topics that usually called for action by the U.S. federal government.

By the early 1970s, speech times had become standardized in both high school and college debate. The four constructive speeches were limited to 10 minutes in college debate and 8 minutes in high school contests, followed by four rebuttals, each half the length of the constructive speeches. Each speaker was cross-examined by an opponent for a 3-minute period following his or her constructive speech. In the late 1980s, Wake Forest University introduced reformed speech times in both its college (9-minute constructives and 6-minute rebuttals) and high school (8 and 5 minutes, respectively) tournaments; these new rules were quickly adopted nationwide.

Topic Selection

High school topic selection is conducted by the National Federation of State High School Associations. Topic proposals are solicited 18 months in advance and are reviewed and discussed at an annual summer meeting (for instance, the meeting to discuss potential topics for 2015–2016 was held in the summer of 2014). The topic meeting creates a ballot of two or three topic choices that are then voted on by schools; the final topic announcement for the coming academic year is made in January.

College topic selection follows a similar process (although the topic is not finalized until the summer before the beginning of the academic year) and is governed by the Cross Examination Debate Association. Some recent high school and college policy topics:

- Resolved: That the United States federal government should substantially increase its economic engagement toward Cuba, Mexico or Venezuela.

- Resolved: That the United States federal government should substantially increase its exploration and/or development of space beyond the Earth's mesosphere.

- Resolved: That the United States federal government should substantially increase its democracy assistance for one or more of the following: Bahrain, Egypt, Libya, Syria, Tunisia, Yemen.

- Resolved: That the United States federal government should substantially reduce its agricultural support, at least eliminating nearly all of the domestic subsidies, for biofuels, concentrated animal feeding operations, corn, cotton, dairy, fisheries, rice, soybeans, sugar and/ or wheat.

Structure

A contemporary high school policy debate round proceeds as follows:

Speech/ Cross-examination	Time	Responsibilities
First Affirmative Constructive (1AC)	8 minutes	Presents the plan and advantages
Cross-examination (CX) of 1AC by 2NC	3 minutes	Clarifies what and how the plan claims to solve; attacks 1AC claims
First Negative Constructive (1NC)	8 minutes	Presents arguments against the plan and advantages (in short form)
CX of 1NC by 1AC	3 minutes	Clarifies claims from 1AC and responds to 1NC claims
Second Affirmative Constructive (2AC)	8 minutes	Responds to negative objections
CX of 2AC by 1NC	3 minutes	Refutes and clarifies 2AC answers

Second Negative Constructive (2NC)	8 minutes	Extends/expands negative arguments, with responses to the second affirmative constructive
CX of 2NC by 2AC	3 minutes	Refutes and clarifies 2NC answers
First Negative Rebuttal (1NR)	5 minutes	Extends negative arguments, with responses to second affirmative constructive
First Affirmative Rebuttal (1AR)	5 minutes	Refutes negative arguments and isolates key arguments required to win
Second Negative Rebuttal (2NR)	5 minutes	Crystallizes the important counterarguments
Second Affirmative Rebuttal (2AR)	5 minutes	Responds to negative crystallization; reinforces plan and advantages

The second negative constructive and the first negative rebuttal constitute the "negative block." Both speakers are answering arguments made by the second affirmative constructive, but they divide their labor: the 2NC discusses certain specific issues, and the 1NR addresses others.

Constructive speeches build or "construct" the basic argu-ments of the debate; each constructive speech is followed by a 3-minute cross-examination period in which the speaker answers questions from the opponent who is not about to speak. For instance, the second negative speaker questions the first affirmative speaker; the first affirmative speaker questions the first negative speaker; and so on.

Rebuttal speeches consolidate and crystallize the most important arguments of the debate. Because the rebuttal speeches are much shorter than constructives, an effec-tive negative team will abandon arguments that they are probably not winning in order to concentrate time on more promising issues.

Depending on the tournament, each team has between 5 and 10 minutes of preparation time, which they may use as they like between speeches. Debaters generally keep time for each other, although the judge may also be keep-ing track of the time.

A college policy debate round has the same structure, but with 9-minute constructive speeches and 6-minute rebut-tal speeches.

Delivery and Style

American Policy Debate often features rapid delivery, although the speed varies by league and region. Judges on many local circuits, and at certain national tourna-ments, still prefer that the debate be conducted at or near conversational speed. Policy debaters speak very quickly— sometimes, between 350 and 500 words per minute—in order to offer as much evidence and make as many arguments as possible during the time allotted.

This style of rapid delivery remains controversial. Many critics believe that increased quantity and diversity of argumentation make debates more educational, while a slower style is preferred by those who want debates to be understandable to lay people and who maintain that the pedagogical purpose of the activity is to train in and hone rhetorical skills. Many further claim that the increased speed encourages debaters to make several poor arguments as opposed to a few high-quality ones. Most debaters will vary their rate of delivery depending on the judge's preferences.

Policy debate is one of the least formal styles of debate. Students often dress casually. Debaters often prompt their partners or interrupt their speeches to clarify arguments. Musical or video presentations are occasionally incorporated into affirmative cases or negative refutation. Increasingly, debaters ask each other questions outside cross-examination, and speakers freely examine each other's evidence (and allow the judge to examine the evidence after the round). Judges often disclose their decisions after rounds and discuss the issues of the debate extensively with the debaters. Debaters may also question judges before rounds about their philosophy or argument preferences. Policy debate has many *conventions*—for instance, that there should be no new arguments in the last speeches or that the affirmative must present a specific plan of action—but few actual *rules*.

Common Arguments

The affirmative team supports the debate resolution by presenting a specific plan of action. For instance, if the resolution were "The United States federal government should substantially increase its economic engagement with Mexico," affirmative debaters would not attempt to defend all types of economic engagement with Mexico in an 8- or 9-minute speech; rather, they would isolate a specific economic project and attempt to demonstrate its benefits. The affirmative might argue that American investment in Mexican energy production would provide cheaper, cleaner energy for both countries or that it would boost the Mexican economy and thereby reduce the number of Mexican immigrants.

The negative team would then present several different types of refutation. First, they might argue that the affirmative actually creates no unique advantage—because their plan cannot achieve its goals or because cheaper energy increases pollution and reduced immigration would cripple American agriculture. Second, the negative could argue that the affirmative plan creates unintended harmful consequences or disadvantages—strains on the U.S. economy or increased political instability in Mexico. Third, the negative might present a counterproposal, or counterplan, to solve the problem the affirmative has identified. Examples might include international action, rather than U.S. action, to create the advantages that the affirmative claims. Finally, the negative might offer a Kritik argument. They might argue that the affirmative proposal should be rejected because it is philosophically unacceptable—that it is an example of an invidious ideology, such as colonialism or imperialism.

All arguments in policy debate rounds are supported with evidence from qualified sources. Brief quotations (called "cards") from books and articles are read verbatim as support. A constructive speech may contain as many as 20 to 30 such cards. Debaters will often make arguments challenging the qualifications of opponents' sources or question the quality or relevance of particular pieces of evidence. Judges often read cards after rounds as they attempt to make a decision.

Additionally, debaters often present theory arguments—reasons why an opponent's strategy or arguments are in some way unfair or inadmissible. The most common theory argument, always advanced by the negative team, is topicality—a claim that the affirmative proposal is not, in fact, an example of the current debate resolution and should, therefore, be rejected. An affirmative team, on the other hand, might argue that a negative counterproposal intrudes on affirmative ground. Either team might argue that an opponent's strategy makes an opposing argument impossible, that the other team's advocacy is impermissibly vague, or that certain arguments have been introduced too late in the debate and should be disregarded. Theory arguments are often presented as voting issues—reasons why the other team should lose the round, independent of any advantages or disadvantages.

Judging

A policy debate tournament consists of a number of preliminary rounds of competition, usually followed by elimination rounds—a series of "sudden death" competitions for teams who performed best in preliminary rounds. These continue until two remaining teams compete in a final round. Usually, single judges decide the outcome of preliminary rounds, while panels of judges (three, five, or seven) decide elimination rounds. Judges are sometimes ordinary citizens with no special knowledge or expertise. More often, they are debate coaches or former debaters with significant debate expertise and topic knowledge. Debaters will adapt their arguments and speaking style to the type of judge assigned to the round.

The judge acts as a disinterested observer who has consciously cast aside his own opinions and preconceptions about the debaters' arguments. He must select a winner based on the arguments and evidence that have actually been presented in the round. To choose a winner, a judge must evaluate each line of argument in detail and ultimately determine whether the affirmative proposal, if theoretically acceptable, would do more harm than good. Judges frequently consult the evidence presented by the debaters as well their own notes from the debate. In deciding, the judge will consider such questions as:

- Where there is direct clash on important issues, which team has the superior evidence and/or explanation?

- Has a team fully explained why their arguments matter, i.e., the impact of their advantages or disadvantages? If the negative has proved that the plan will cause disadvantages, do they outweigh the advantages of the plan?

- Has a team simply failed to answer an important opposing argument?

Although some tournaments forbid judges from disclosing their decisions immediately following the round, most very competitive tournaments encourage post-round inter-action between the judge and debaters, with the judge announcing the decision, explaining the rationale, and answering questions that the debaters may wish to ask.

The judge must also award speaker points to each compet-itor. The decision and the awarding of points are largely independent processes. Speaker points are a more sub-jective evaluation of each debater's skills. Speaker point formulas vary throughout local, state, and regional organizations, particularly at the high school level. Most tournaments use values ranging from 0 to 30. In practice, points below 25 are reserved for extremely poor perfor-mances, while a perfect score of 30 is rare and warranted only by a truly outstanding performance. Generally, speaker points are seen as less important than wins and losses. Judges may, and sometimes do, give fewer speaker points to the winning team than to the losing team. Most tournaments also present debaters with speaker awards—recognition for debaters who received the highest point totals in the tournament.

BRITISH PARLIAMENTARY DEBATE

Overview

British Parliamentary (BP) Debate is probably the most commonly used format in the world, with major support in the United Kingdom, Ireland, continental Europe, Africa, Philippines, and the United States. It has also been adopted as the official style of the World Universities Debating Championship and the European Universities Debating Championship and, as a result, is the default format for many university debating societies. In some areas, it is used along with a regional or local format.

BP is loosely based on the traditions of the British Parliament and retains some of the conventions of the House of Commons. For example, the two sides are Government (or Proposition) and Opposition, and debaters offer points of information (POIs) similar to the interruptions made by members of Parliament, to comment or raise a question about their opponent's arguments.

British Parliamentary Debate is unique among other parliamentary formats in that it calls for four teams of two speakers each—two teams for the Government and two for the Opposition. Teams compete both against the other side of the House and the other team on their side. Each team is trying to win the debate for themselves. This organization creates an unusual dynamic because the two teams on each side must work together while also trying to best the other. Because BP has limited preparation (the motion is usually introduced 15 minutes before the debate), the format emphasizes quick thinking and a good knowledge of a wide range of subjects.

History

University debating societies began in the early nineteenth century; some of the first were at St. Andrew's, Cambridge, and Oxford. These first debates were predominantly intramural and were modeled very directly on the style and substance of actual debate in Parliament. The Cambridge and Oxford unions, in particular, often invited political figures to participate in their debates. Occasionally debaters from other universities would be invited to participate. Tournaments which invited many universities to attend (and bring multiple teams), are a postwar innovation, as are standardized formats and speech times.

Topic Selection

Because of the geographic range of the format, the motions vary significantly between countries. As in other formats, politics, economics, and current and foreign affairs dominate, but any subject can be debated. There is a growing trend toward introducing more esoteric subjects and providing information slides to allow debaters to brief themselves on the pertinent facts.

Structure

The distinguishing characteristic of British Parliamentary Debate is the use of two teams on each side, making four speakers for the Government and four for the Opposition. Each debater speaks only once; there are no reply speeches. Each team's position in the debate is drawn at random just before the debate begins.

The debate proceeds as follows:

Opening Government	Opening Opposition
1. Prime Minister	2. Leader of the Opposition
3. Deputy Prime Minister	4. Deputy Leader of the Opposition

Closing Government	Closing Opposition
5. Member for the Government	6. Member for the Opposition
7. Government Whip	8. Opposition Whip

Team roles are split into two categories, those for the *opening* factions, and those for the *closing* factions. The Opening Government defines the motion, presents its case, and responds to arguments from the Opposition. The Opening Opposition introduces their arguments and critiques the Government's case. It does not offer a counter-proposal. The Closing Government provides an extension and summarizes the Government's position. The Closing Opposition addresses the arguments put forth both in the extension and at the top of the debate. All teams work to remain relevant throughout the debate.

Speaking times vary from country to country and tournament to tournament, but are generally between 5 and 7 minutes for each speech. Occasionally, the speaking order varies. For example, in New Zealand, both the leader of the Opposition and the prime minister offer a short summary as the last two speakers.

The format is challenging because each of the four teams is trying to win the debate both for their side and for their team. Each team of two works separately, not in conjunction with the other team on their side. In effect, the teams on each side form a coalition, working to reach the same conclusion on the motion but from slightly different perspectives.

Delivery and Style

The British Parliamentary format generally emphasizes eloquence and the use of humor, but whether substance or style matter most depends on the region. Etiquette also varies by region. In some areas, the opening teams are encouraged to present as many arguments as possible, thus leaving little for the closing teams to add. In some regions, this is strongly discouraged. BP also permits heckling—critical and occasionally sarcastic interruptions by opponents.

Important Features

A feature unique to BP is the use of extensions, the introduction of a major new platform of argument by the Closing Government team. Generally, extensions are in accordance with the case presented by the Opening Government team but examine the issue from a new perspective. The extension does not start an entirely new debate. Instead, it proves the truth of the motion for different reasons.

Points of information are particularly important in British Parliamentary style, as they allow the first two teams to maintain their relevance during the course of the debate, and the last two teams to introduce their arguments early in the debate. The first and last minute of each speech is considered "protected time" during which no POI may be offered.

Judging

Judging is done by a panel of adjudicators. The four-team format makes simply voting for the best team impossible as no team might receive enough votes to win. And the three other teams must be ranked. Consequently, decisions are made by consensus. Judges evaluate structure and style and look for arguments supported by examples and analysis. They want to see good rebuttal of an opposing team's arguments and the effective use of POIs.

CONGRESSIONAL DEBATE

Overview

Congressional Debate involves students emulating members of the U.S. Congress by debating legislation that the participants have prepared ahead of time. Sometimes referred to as "Mock Congress," "Student Congress," or "legislative debate," it is a popular American debate format offered by the National Speech and Debate Association (NSDA), the National Catholic Forensic League, and most state leagues.

Congressional Debate is possibly the most well-rounded activity in speech and debate. It offers students the opportunity to choose and debate topics that are of particular interest to them, research issues in depth, show off their speaking skills, and experience U.S. congressional procedure.

Congressional Debate requires a broad, deep knowledge of current events, the ability to communicate clearly and concisely to a general audience, and strategic knowledge of parliamentary procedure. Successful Congressional debaters are assertive, but not aggressive; they must also be cooperative, since the passage of legislation frequently involves building coalitions with other senators or representatives.

History

Intercollegiate model Congresses, sponsored by the college honorary society Pi Kappa Delta, were held as early as 1917. These Congresses debated actual legislation that the U.S. Congress was considering at the time. The first national high school Congressional Debate was held in 1938 by the National Forensic League (now the National Speech and Debate Association).

For many years the format was relatively noncompetitive in that first-, second-, and third-place winners were not declared. Instead, awards were presented to "superior" or "outstanding" members and presiding officers from each chamber. Beginning in the 1980s, judges used rank and point systems to create semifinal and final rounds, along with ordinal awards (first, second, etc.) for outstanding debaters.

Congressional Debate has grown steadily since 2000. Beginning with the Harvard tournament and the Tournament of Champions in 2002, many large national invitational tournaments, as well as state tournaments, have added the format.

Structure

Students in Congressional Debate act as members of Congress who draft, revise, and amend bills and resolutions; they then debate those measures and vote on whether to enact them. Participating teams may enter students in the House of Representatives, the Senate, or both. Most large tournaments divide the House and Senate into chambers of 15–20 students.

Before the event, each school submits mock legislation to each tournament. Tournaments may review the submissions before sharing the overall docket with participating schools. Contestants from each school then research and prepare arguments for and against each item in the docket.

Legislation

Students themselves create the topics for each Congressional Debate contest by submitting proposed bills and resolutions. Legislation must address a national or international issue and must fall within congressional jurisdiction. Examples of Congressional Debate bills and resolutions might include:

- Legislation that would reestablish a U.S. federal government assault weapons ban.

- Legislation increasing the federal minimum wage.

- Legislation revising minimum nutritional standards for school lunches.

- A resolution calling for the resignation of a member of the Cabinet.

- A bill or resolution calling for an amendment to the Constitution.

BILLS

Bills are concise, legally precise statements of legislative action, usually divided into sections, as shown in the following example:

BE IT ENACTED BY THE STUDENT CONGRESS
HERE ASSEMBLED THAT:

SECTION 1. The National Railroad Passenger
Corporation, or Amtrak, shall be privatized.

SECTION 2. Privatization of Amtrak is defined
as changing from government to publically
traded control and ownership through the
sale of preferred stock and de-federalizing the
appointment of Amtrak's board of directors.

SECTION 3. The Department of Transportation will oversee the enforcement of this Bill,
which is binding to all parties in agreement to
Section 1 and has the same effect as if arrived
at by agreement of the parties under the Rail-
way Labor Act.

SECTION 4. Amtrak's preferred stock will
be saleable upon passage of this Bill and
Amtrak's board of directors managed by the
corporation's owners.

SECTION 5. All laws in conflict with this legislation are hereby declared null and void.

RESOLUTIONS

A resolution, in contrast, simply expresses an opinion for
the House or Senate to affirm. A resolution usually begins
by presenting a series of brief justifications for the change
being advocated, followed by a statement of the change
that the House or Senate supports:

A resolution to ban a cap-and-trade policy

WHEREAS a cap-and-trade system necessarily harms the economy because it is designed to raise the cost of energy, and

WHEREAS given the current economic crisis, an expensive energy policy is a bad idea, and

WHEREAS almost all acts of economic production are powered by combusting fossil fuels, and

WHEREAS a cap-and-trade policy initiated by the United States would not bring a reduction in greenhouse gases by China or India.

THEREFORE BE IT RESOLVED by this Student Congress here assembled that the United States federal government should not implement a cap-and-trade system.

The Competition

Students register for either the House or the Senate. The Senate has a smaller number of contestants; usually these are the more experienced. Debaters attending each tournament are divided into sections of 15–20, called "chambers." The debaters compete in one or more rounds, or sessions. A session customarily allows 10 minutes per competing student—an average of three hours. Larger tournaments may have elimination rounds (semifinals, finals); smaller tournaments may omit elimination rounds and simply present awards to students with the highest scores in individual chambers.

At the beginning of each session, each chamber elects a presiding officer, or chair, by secret ballot. The presiding officer's main job is to facilitate debate by calling on speakers and questioners according to the guidelines set by the tournament. He or she will also recognize speakers who wish to make motions, enforce time limits on speeches and questions, count votes on motions or legislation, and, with the assistance of the parliamentarian, make certain that parliamentary procedure is followed.

Congressional Debate speeches last up to 3 minutes. The first speech on each piece of legislation, known as the "authorship speech," goes to the debater who wrote the legislation, or, if the author is not present, to another debater from the author's school. This first speech is followed by a 2-minute questioning period. One 3-minute speech in opposition follows, with another 2-minute questioning period. After these initial speeches, speakers who support the legislation alternate with speakers who oppose it; each speaker is allotted 3 minutes, followed by 1 minute of questioning time. A typical speech develops two or three brief arguments supported by statistics or reference to expert opinion. Typically, questions attempt to expose faults in the speech. Sometimes speakers upholding the same side as the current speaker will ask a "friendly question," seeking agreement. Judges expect questions and answers to be concise; students should not include a statement or argument as part of their question.

As debate proceeds, the presiding officer will first recognize those who have not spoken or those who have spoken least (this practice is referred to as "precedence"). Many leagues also require the presiding officer to prefer debaters who have not spoken recently (this practice is referred to as "recency").

As debate continues, students present motions: for example, to amend the bill, to table it, or to close debate so that a vote may be taken. The presiding officer then guides the chamber according to principles of parliamentary procedure. The National Forensic League's Table of Parliamentary Motions (excerpted below), adapted from *Robert's Rules of Order*, is generally used as a Congressional Debate standard for procedure.

Frequently Used Parliamentary Motions

Motion	Notes	Second Required	Fraction of Chamber Required
To open the floor to debate	Also called the "main motion"	Yes	Majority
To take a bill from the table	Reopens debate on tabled legislation, which may or may not have already been debated	Yes	Majority
To lay a bill on the table	Pauses debate on a bill. Some states typically return to vote on all tabled items before the conclusion of a tournament, but there is no rule requiring this	Yes	Majority

Motion	Notes	Second Required	Fraction of Chamber Required
To call the previous question	To call the previous question ends debate on a bill and states the main motion to vote on it	Yes	2/3
To recess	Length of the recess (e.g., "for 10 minutes," "until 11:30") must be specified	Yes	Majority
To rise to a point of personal privilege	To make a personal request	No	Decision of chair
To rise to a point of order/ parliamentary procedure	To correct a parliamentary error, ask a question, or clarify a procedure	No	Decision of chair
To amend	Modifies a pending motion or the pending bill/resolution; filled-out slip must be passed to presiding officer in advance	Yes	2/3 majority to call the previous question to end debate, then majority to pass
To adjourn	Made at the end of a tournament	Yes	Majority

These motions are allowed at some Congressional Debate tournaments, depending on the region and the style of debate:

Motion	Notes	Second Required	Fraction of Chamber Required
To demand a roll call vote	Used to verify a voice vote or vote by show of hands	Yes	1/5
To "divide the house"	Used to verify a voice vote	No	Demand by a single member requires a re-count.
To modify or withdraw a motion	To change or take back a motion that has not yet been passed	Yes, only if chair has already stated the motion	Majority (after motion is stated by chair), no vote required if motion has not been stated
To suspend the rules	To take an action against rules (such as adding an additional minute of questioning)	Yes	2/3

To appeal a decision of the chair	Allows chamber to overrule the presiding officer's ruling on a prior point of order	Yes	Majority
To extend questioning time	To continue asking questions of the speaker	Yes	2/3

Once debate has been closed, the presiding officer calls for a vote on the legislation and, after counting votes, announces whether the motion is carried or is defeated.

Students may propose amendments in writing to the presiding officer. If the presiding officer decides that the amendment is germane or directly relevant to the legislation, the author of the amendment may then move to amend, reading the amendment aloud to the chamber. If one-third of the chamber agrees to consider the amendment, the presiding officer then calls for a speech in support of the amendment, and debate continues until the previous question is moved. Once the amendment passes, fails, is tabled, or is withdrawn, debate returns to the main bill or resolution.

The Parliamentarian

In addition to judges who score speeches, most tournaments have an adult parliamentarian in each chamber. Unlike scorers, who generally rotate each session, the parliamentarian remains in one chamber for all sessions (preliminary, semifinal, or final). The parliamentarian's role is to serve as a reference on parliamentary procedure in case confusion or a dispute arises that the presiding officer cannot resolve. Unless the presiding officer makes (or fails to correct) a major error in procedure, the parliamentarian is unlikely to intervene.

Style and Delivery

Congressional Debate is friendly but formal. Boys wear suits and ties; girls wear skirts or business suits. The standard of courtesy is very high. Debaters address each other as "Representative Smith" or "Senator Hardwick." Personal remarks or interruptions are likely to be ruled out of order. Apart from authorship speeches, the discourse is extemporaneous and students speak slowly, at times oratorically.

Judging

Judges in Congressional Debate are often called "scorers." They may be experienced Congressional Debate coaches, coaches of other forensics activities, or community or parent judges. One or more scorers is assigned to each chamber.

Scorers evaluate individual speeches, awarding points on a 1–6 scale, 6 being best. Scorers consider each speaker's command of the subject matter, speaking style, and persuasive ability. While scorers will apply their own criteria, generally they will reward debaters who provide new arguments (rather than repeating those already advanced);

who present credible evidence; who are well-organized; and who speak extemporaneously and fluently.

Scorers also evaluate presiding officers, again using a 1–6 scale. Good presiding officers demonstrate a strong knowledge of parliamentary procedure, firmly but fairly enforce time limits, and communicate clearly and concisely.

Finally, each scorer lists the several best debaters in the chamber in order. In NSDA competitions, a scorer ranks eight debaters, first through eighth; the presiding officer may be included in this ranking.

KARL POPPER DEBATE

Overview

The Karl Popper format, developed by the Open Society Institute (now Open Society Foundations), promulgated by the International Debate Education Association, and named after the famous philosopher Karl Popper, was designed for countries with no modern experience of academic debate. Accordingly, it is most commonly found in Eastern European and Central Asian secondary schools and universities. Its format is a hybrid of policy and parliamentary debate featuring three-person teams who debate current, controversial value or policy topics. All Karl Popper teams switch sides several times in the course of a tournament and so must be prepared to debate both sides of the resolution.

Karl Popper Debate was developed as an educational tool to encourage critical thinking, tolerance for different views, and respect for ethical principles. The format stresses cooperation: each team works and is judged as a unit. In keeping with the format's educational focus, debaters roles are not specialized; team members must work together throughout the debate. The format is often considered a good starting point for high school debaters.

Topic Selection

Each tournament chooses its own topic and announces it approximately one month in advance. Topics may be resolutions of policy or of value, though policy resolutions frequently express an obvious value conflict. A good Karl Popper Debate resolution is highly controversial, addresses current concerns, and directs students to discussion of fundamental moral differences.

A Karl Popper value resolution would make a statement of morality without calling for specific action. It might be a simple resolution ("Capital punishment is immoral.") or a comparative resolution ("Capital punishment is more humane than life imprisonment without the possibility of parole."). A Karl Popper policy resolution would urge a specific government action grounded in a core value ("The nations of the world should abolish capital punishment."). Still other resolutions might present a debatable analogy ("Capital punishment is like murder.") or assert a moral or political relationship ("Capital punishment models and sanctions other forms of brutality.").

Examples of Karl Popper Debate resolutions include:

Resolutions of value

Euthanasia is morally justifiable.

All individuals deserve free medical care.

Governments have no right to monitor citizens' emails.

Governments have a moral obligation to assist political refugees.

Resolutions of policy

Countries should ban the import of goods produced by child labor.

The United Nations should condemn Russia's seizure of the Crimea.

Governments should support net neutrality.

Countries should provide a guaranteed annual income for all citizens.

Structure

In Karl Popper Debate, six individuals speak during each debate. Three affirmative speakers support the resolution; three negative speakers oppose it. The debate is composed of 10 parts: 6 speeches and 4 periods of cross-examination.

Order of Speakers

Speech	Time	Speaker
1. Affirmative Constructive	6 minutes	First Affirmative Speaker
2. Cross-Examination	3 minutes	Third Negative Speaker questions First Affirmative Speaker answers
3. Negative Constructive	6 minutes	First Negative Speaker

Speech	Time	Speaker
4. Cross-Examination	3 minutes	Third Affirmative Speaker questions
		First Negative Speaker answers
5. First Affirmative Rebuttal	5 minutes	Second Affirmative Speaker
6. Cross-Examination	3 minutes	First Negative Speaker questions
		Second Affirmative Speaker answers
7. First Negative Rebuttal	5 minutes	Second Negative Speaker
8. Cross-Examination	3 minutes	First Affirmative Speaker questions
		Second Negative Speaker answers
9. Final Affirmative Rebuttal (Reply)	5 minutes	Third Affirmative Speaker
10. Final Negative Rebuttal (Reply)	5 minutes	Third Negative Speaker

The first two speeches are constructive speeches in which each team presents its basic arguments as well as the evidence and reasoning needed to support them. The first affirmative speaker begins the debate with the team's redefinition or interpretation of the resolution. She may also provide definitions of key terms of the resolution and an overview explaining the affirmative's approach to the topic. She then offers her major arguments in support of the resolution. In a policy debate, for instance, this speaker might provide evidence of the magnitude of the problem in the status quo, prove that the present system is not solving the problem, and offer a solution to the problem. The first negative speaker would contest the affirmative's interpretation of the resolution; she then presents answers to the specific arguments made in the affirmative case. A prepared negative case, or attack on the resolution proper, is not necessary. Negative teams may argue that the problem identified by the affirmative is not as compelling as the affirmative claims or that the proposed solution cannot solve the problem. The negative might also present their own proposed course of action. Generally, all arguments are laid out in the first speeches, with later speakers free to develop them.

The next two speeches are rebuttals in which each side directly refutes the points made by the opposing team. In some Karl Popper formats, the second affirmative speaker may offer additional case arguments.

Each of the first four speeches is followed by a period of cross-examination that is used to clarify arguments, expose fallacies or weaknesses in opposing arguments, highlight the absence of evidence or warrants, and lay the groundwork for objections that will be made in subsequent speeches.

The final rebuttal, or reply speeches, attempt to crystallize each team's position. The affirmative reply speaker responds to any new material that the second negative speaker introduced and may also defend the affirmative case using new evidence; but her major goal is to focus the adjudicator on the decision she wants him to reach. She will drop extraneous arguments and emphasize those key to the debate—the points of clash. She also aims to establish the criterion by which the debate should be judged by urging the adjudicator to consider one factor or perspective as being paramount.

The last negative speaker need not address the affirmative team's summary—his team's rebuttalist has done that already. Instead, he summarizes the negative case and then addresses the key issues in the debate, showing why the negative's position is superior in every instance.

The debaters are expected to support arguments with warrants and appropriate evidence. On some topics, debaters may use examples and appeals to common knowledge, but research is important in this format. Statistics from reputable sources and conclusions from experts in the field are often used—quoted verbatim and cited.

Each debate includes several minutes of preparation time—usually between 3 and 5 minutes per team, although the amount varies from country to country. In some countries, the negative team has more prep time than the affirmative team. Teams may take preparation time in increments—for example, 1 minute before the rebuttal, and the rest before the reply speech. Cross-examination can also be valuable preparation time for debaters who are not engaged in the cross-examination.

Variations of the format have evolved in different countries. The length of speeches, length of prep time during the debate, point system for evaluation, and sometimes even the notes for adjudicators may vary. Many Karl Popper formats now allow for a second affirmative speaker to introduce a new argument, although in practice this happens very rarely.

Delivery and Style

Karl Popper Debate adheres to high standards of courtesy, accessibility, and educational value. Speakers frequently compliment their opponents' speeches. Arguments must appeal to a general audience. Arguments designed to gain competitive advantage at the expense of clarity or reasonability are seldom rewarded.

Unique Features

In many styles of debate, the words "refutation" and "rebuttal" are synonymous: both refer to answers given to opposing argument. In Karl Popper Debate, the terms are distinct. "Refutation" is a general term, meaning response to arguments made by the opposing team. "Rebuttal" refers specifically to the process undertaken by the second speakers to address the arguments of the first speakers.

Additionally, Karl Popper debaters are trained in a specific five-point system of refutation. A response to any given argument should include:

1. *Reference*: Identify exactly which of your opponent's arguments you are addressing

2. *Response*: Specify the problem with the argument

3. *Support*: Cite or introduce evidence to support your contention that your preferred alternative is superior

4. *Explanation*: Demonstrate logically that the evidence speaks directly to the argument in question and justifies your claim of a superior position

5. *Impact*: This stage is optional, but you may explain why this argument is of significance to the wider debate and why it benefits your team

Karl Popper Debate assumes that refutation will emphasize an alternative argument or position, rather than simply offer a criticism of an opponent's argument. A negative debater might note, for instance, that an affirmative argument lacks supporting evidence; he would be expected to provide counterargument and counterevidence as well.

Judging

Like other debate judges, adjudicators in Karl Popper Debate base their decision on the argumentation and evidence introduced in the course of the debate and work hard to ignore any biases they may have on the topic. Karl Popper Debate emphasizes training in thinking and analysis; of course, good speaking is rewarded, but logic and structure are more important than communicative style. Although there are sometimes panels of adjudicators, it is not uncommon for Karl Popper debates to be judged by a sole adjudicator. Adjudicators are required to provide constructive feedback on the debate, not simply announce the winner. Additionally, the adjudicator keeps time for the debaters and is responsible for maintaining a positive, collegial atmosphere during the debate round.

LINCOLN–DOUGLAS DEBATE

Overview

Lincoln–Douglas Debate (LD) is a one-on-one debate format that is extremely popular in U.S. high schools. It is also a college event, mostly at tournaments sponsored by the National Forensic Association. The format is named after Abraham Lincoln and Stephen Douglas, who engaged in a famous series of one-on-one debates during their 1858 campaign for the U.S. Senate. Lincoln–Douglas debates usually focus on a proposition of value—whether one quality, principle, or policy should be preferred to another or whether a particular course of action is morally justified. A Lincoln–Douglas resolution might ask whether liberty is more important than equality, whether environmental protection should take precedence over economic growth, or whether the possession of nuclear weapons is moral. Debaters must be prepared to argue either side of the resolution and will defend the affirmative and negative sides an equal number of times in any given tournament.

Lincoln–Douglas debaters prepare by studying moral and political philosophy; they also do substantial research on each specific topic. Most LD debaters participate in local or regional tournaments, but a small number, usually from elite schools, take part in national circuit tournaments.

History

For most of the twentieth century, most interscholastic debates in the United States involved teams of two or more students; "Lincoln–Douglas" became a generic term for any type of contest between single debaters. LD was occasionally offered as a specialty event at high school and college tournaments, but had no standard format. Policy debate remained predominant, particularly at the high school level.

As policy debaters began to speak more and more quickly and offer more technical arguments, many traditional high school coaches began to look for an alternative, audience-friendly debate format. In 1981, the National Forensic League (now the National Speech and Debate Association, or NSDA) adopted Lincoln–Douglas Debate as a national event, with the now-standard speaker order and speech times. By the end of the decade, most state debate leagues had adopted Lincoln–Douglas as a standard event, and LD quickly overtook policy debate in popularity. All major national high school tournaments, including the National Catholic Forensic League Grand National tournament and the National Debate Coaches Association tournament, now offer Lincoln–Douglas. Collegiate Lincoln–Douglas Debate is confined primarily to tournaments affiliated with the National Forensic Association.

Lincoln–Douglas Debate has undergone rapid change in recent years. Originally, it was a distinct event that stressed communication with a general audience. Since 2000, its scope has expanded to include a wider range of philosophical arguments, including European and postmodern perspectives. Lincoln–Douglas resolutions are sometimes indistinguishable from American Policy Debate resolutions, and LD has absorbed many policy arguments, including affirmative plans, disadvantages, counterplans, and theory arguments. In a sense, LD has become the most inclusive of debate styles, offering the widest variety of argument styles and judging perspectives; but it has also become more demanding of debaters and judges alike.

Topic Selection

High school Lincoln–Douglas topic selection is sponsored by the National Speech and Debate Association. Anyone may submit a topic. A committee of senior educators meets each June at the NSDA national tournament, considers possible problem areas and resolutions, and produces a list of 10 possible topics for the coming school year. Member schools vote on these topics, and ultimately five resolutions are chosen, one for each of four two-month periods (September–October, November–December, January–February, and March–April) and one for the NSDA national tournament. Other high school national championship tournaments may adopt one of the NSDA topics for their contests or choose their own unique resolution. Intercollegiate Lincoln–Douglas topic selection follows a similar process, except that only one topic is selected for use throughout the year.

In 2013, NSDA offered a special introductory Lincoln–Douglas resolution for novice high school debaters ("Resolved: That civil disobedience in a democracy is morally justified."). NSDA intends it as a recurring September–October topic that schools and leagues might use to train beginners in fundamental political philosophy.

Recent high school resolutions include:

- Resolved: Just governments ought to ensure food security for their citizens.

- Resolved: Just governments ought to require that employers pay a living wage.

- Resolved: The "right to be forgotten" from Internet searches ought to be a civil right.

- Resolved: A just society ought to presume consent for organ procurement from the deceased.

Collegiate resolutions have included:

- Resolved: The United States federal government should substantially increase assistance for organic and/or sustainable agriculture in the United States.

- Resolved: The United States federal government should substantially change its trade policy and/or practices with the People's Republic of China.

Structure

A Lincoln–Douglas round proceeds as follows:

Speech	Time	Responsibilities
Affirmative Constructive	6 minutes	Presents the Affirmative case

Cross-examination	3 minutes	Negative speaker asks questions; Affirmative speaker responds
Negative Constructive	7 minutes	Presents the Negative case; followed by refutation of Affirmative case
Cross-examination	3 minutes	Affirmative speaker asks questions; Negative speaker responds
First Affirmative Rebuttal	4 minutes	Answers the Negative case and extends the Affirmative case; responds to Negative refutation
Negative Rebuttal	6 minutes	Answers the first Affirmative rebuttal; highlights reasons to vote Negative
Second Affirmative Rebuttal	3 minutes	Highlights reasons to vote Affirmative; incorporates answers to Negative rebuttal

The affirmative debater spends all of his constructive time delivering his prepared case, which typically includes definitions of key terms in the resolution; a statement of the basic philosophical value he supports; and a value criterion, which presents the judge with a method of deciding whether the debater has upheld his value. These are followed by the debater's major arguments, or contentions, usually supported by evidence from expert sources.

A traditional negative case is also prepared in advance, but it is usually about 4 minutes long—leaving the rest of the constructive speech time for specific attacks on the affirmative case.

Rebuttal speeches consolidate and crystallize the most important arguments of the debate. Because the rebuttal speeches are much shorter than the constructives, an effective negative debater will abandon arguments that she is probably not winning to concentrate on more promising issues.

Each debater has between 3 and 5 minutes of preparation time (tournament and league rules vary) to use as she or he sees fit during the round. Some tournaments and judges permit the use of "flex prep," in which debaters may apply cross-examination time to prep time or vice versa. For instance, a debater using flex prep might spend only a minute asking questions and use the other 2 minutes for preparation; conversely, she might continue to ask questions during her preparation time. Debaters generally keep time for each other, although the judge may also keep track of the time.

Most speeches start with an "order" that states the sequence in which the arguments will be addressed (e.g., "It's going to be the affirmative constructive, then the theory arguments, then the negative constructive, and, finally, the disadvantage argument.").

Delivery and Style

Lincoln–Douglas began as a reaction against the perceived excesses of policy debate—in particular, fast speaking and the use of technical debate language. Traditional Lincoln–Douglas Debate is still conducted at or slightly above conversational speed and is centered (insofar as possible) on values arguments rather than policy arguments. National circuit Lincoln–Douglas, on the other hand, has adopted many practices—rapid delivery, the use of technical language, and the proliferation of arguments, including disadvantages, counterplans, and theory arguments—that until recently were only found in American Policy Debate rounds. Lincoln–Douglas debaters generally dress more formally than policy debaters.

Common Arguments

Traditional Lincoln–Douglas cases are logical syllogisms that attempt to prove the resolution true or false or show the desirability or undesirability of the affirmative or negative. A typical traditional case consists of a framework, which outlines the conditions for discussing the resolution, and contentions. The most essential part of the framework is the value structure, which is composed of an ultimate value (often called the "value premise") and which the case attempts to demonstrate the resolutional action achieves/is in accordance with, and a value criterion (also called the "standard"), which provides a method of determining whether the value has been achieved. Depending on the topic, morality, justice, social welfare, and liberty are common values. The framework also may contain definitions that clarify terms of the resolution or attempt to limit or expand the scope of the resolution. The framework is followed by contentions, or major arguments, that link the resolution to the value structure. A contention necessarily includes a claim, which summarizes the argument; at least one warrant, which is a reason the claim is true; and an impact, which explains the importance of the argument—or, specifically, why this argument meets the value criterion.

For example, an affirmative case for the resolution "Resolved: That the death penalty is a morally justified form of punishment" could have a value of justice, a value criterion of crime deterrence, and then contentions, supported by statistical and possibly psychological evidence, that demonstrate that the death penalty serves as a uniquely powerful deterrent. A negative case could feature a value of justice, a criterion of respecting human worth, and contentions arguing that the killing of human beings is unacceptable for any reason, regardless of any crimes that those human beings might have committed. It could also argue that all presently available methods of execution are inhumane (lethal injection is believed to be physically painful and psychologically traumatizing, while hanging, electrocution, and gassing certainly are). The debaters would then argue whether practical crime deterrence or adherence to the principle of human worth is more important to justice and if each other's contentions sufficiently meet even their own value criterion.

Increasingly, Lincoln–Douglas cases are departing from this traditional format. On some circuits, affirmative cases may resemble policy debate cases, with plans that outline examples of resolutional action and contentions devoted to proving policy stock issues (harm, inherency, and solvency). Negative debaters may simply omit presenting their own case and devote the full 7 minutes of constructive time to refutation, which may include counterplans, disadvantages, and theoretical arguments. Kritik arguments are increasingly popular in Lincoln–Douglas on both sides of the resolution.

Judging

Because Lincoln–Douglas debates are about half as long as policy debates, judges are usually assigned to hear two flights of rounds per time block, with the second round beginning immediately after the first has concluded. These rounds are designated as "Flight A" and "Flight B." Half of a tournament's debaters will compete in Flight A, the other half in Flight B. Typically Lincoln–Douglas debaters have four to seven preliminary rounds of competition, followed by elimination rounds—a series of "sudden death" competitions for teams who performed best in preliminary rounds. These continue until the two remaining teams compete in a final round. Generally, single judges decide the outcome of preliminary rounds, while panels of judges (three, five, or seven) decide elimination rounds.

Judges are sometimes ordinary citizens with no special knowledge or expertise. More often, they are debate coaches or former debaters with significant debate expertise and topic knowledge. Debaters will adapt their arguments and speaking style to the judge assigned to the round. Because judges vary widely in their backgrounds and stylistic preferences, debaters will often ask judges to discuss their judging philosophy before the round begins.

The judge acts as a disinterested observer who has consciously cast aside her own opinions and preconceptions regarding the debaters' arguments. She must select a winner based on the arguments and evidence that are actually presented in the round.

To choose a winner, a judge must evaluate each line of argument in detail and ultimately determine whether the affirmative position, if theoretically acceptable, would do more harm than good. Judges sometimes consult the evidence presented by the debaters as well their own notes from the debate. In deciding, the judge will consider such questions as:

- Which value premise is more compelling? If the debaters offer similar value premises, which side promotes that value better?

- Where there is direct clash on important issues, which team has the superior evidence and/or explanation?

- Which debater has more fully explained why her arguments matter, i.e., the impact of the arguments?

- Has a team simply failed to answer an important opposing argument?

Additionally, the judge must award speaker points to each competitor. The decision and the awarding of points are largely independent processes. An excellent speaker who is less talented at argument than his opponent might get higher points but lose the decision; or, a debater might display more all-around skill than her opponent yet mishandle a critical argument.

Speaker points are a more subjective evaluation of each debater's skills. Speaker point formulas vary throughout local state and regional organizations, particularly at the high school level. Most tournaments use values ranging from 0 to 30. In practice, points below 25 are reserved for extremely poor performances, while a perfect score of 30 is rare and warranted only by a truly outstanding performance. Generally, speaker points are seen as less important than wins and losses. Judges may, and sometimes do, give fewer speaker points to the winning team than to the losing team. Most tournaments also present debaters with speaker awards—recognition for debaters who received the highest point totals in the tournament.

MOCK TRIAL

Overview

Mock Trial is a competitive event in which students assume the roles of attorneys and witnesses in either a criminal or civil trial. Teams will prepare arguments for one or both sides (prosecution or plaintiff, and defendant) of a given case (depending on the level of competition). A packet with the facts of the case to be tried, affidavits (written transcripts of testimony), and exhibits (objects, photographs, or documents) is made available to competing teams in advance of the tournament. Some team members act as attorneys; others play the role of witnesses. The teams then simulate an actual trial, which follows the rules of civil or criminal procedure, with an adult adjudicator playing the role of courtroom judge. The cases are written in an attempt to create an equal chance of either side prevailing, since the main objective is not to identify the winner of the case but, rather, the team with superior advocacy skills.

The competition is designed to educate students in legal research, reasoning, legal procedure, and oral advocacy. Different kinds of Mock Trial competitions are offered at the grade school, middle school, high school, and university level; they are most common in the United States, but are also found in Canada, Australia, Asia, and the United Kingdom.

United States Mock Trial

History and Governing Bodies

Mock Trial competitions have been held for many years in the United States, but standardized national competition is relatively new. The first National High School Mock Trial Championship was held in 1984. The event has grown each year, and now has national representation; different participating states take turns hosting the tournament. Intercollegiate Mock Trial competition is governed by the American Mock Trial Association (AMTA), which was founded in 1985. AMTA hosts 25 regional tournaments, eight opening round championship tournaments, and a national championship tournament season. Approximately 600 teams from more than 350 universities and colleges compete in these events. In total, AMTA provides a forum for more than 5,300 undergraduate students each academic year to engage in intercollegiate Mock Trial competitions across the country. Additionally, it provides case materials for use by local and regional competitions.

Levels of Competition

COLLEGIATE

A college Mock Trial team has six persons. In any given Mock Trial round, three team members act as attorneys and three prepare to play roles as witnesses. Each team may be assigned the role of plaintiff/prosecution or defense in any given round. Each school may enter any number of six-person teams. The attorneys are responsible for delivering an opening statement, conducting direct and cross-examinations of witnesses, and delivering closing arguments. Witnesses consist of experts as well as lay witnesses. Judges are usually attorneys or coaches; on occasion, sitting judges will agree to serve as judges for Mock Trial.

The first case packet of the season is generally written and distributed prior to the beginning of the scholastic year in August, with new cases appearing throughout the season, usually in September, December, and, finally, in February. The February packet is used for the national championship. All collegiate Mock Trial cases take place in the fictional U.S. state of Midlands and thus fall under the protection of the U.S. Constitution.

A collegiate Mock Trial tournament has four rounds of competition. Each team acts as prosecution in two rounds and as defense in the other two rounds. A complete Mock Trial round takes approximately 3 hours. Each round is heard by either two or three judges, who independently choose a winning team and assign quality points to individual contestants. The tournament season has two parts: the invitational season, which lasts throughout the fall semester and into the early spring semester, and the regular season, which consists of regional tournaments that precede the national tournament—it runs from late January into April.

HIGH SCHOOL

High school Mock Trial differs from collegiate Mock Trial in that participating schools debate one case for the regular season. To prepare for competition, teams thoroughly read and analyze the case packet. Additionally, high school

Mock Trial is governed by state bar associations, thus cases, rules, and competition structure vary from state to state (unlike college Mock Trial, which argues the same cases under the same rules nationwide). The winners of state competitions then advance to the National High School Mock Trial Competition, which is held each May, and which offers a unique topic with new case materials.

ELEMENTARY AND MIDDLE SCHOOL COMPETITION

Most elementary school Mock Trial competitions are intramural or classroom exercises. Most often, students assume roles in scripted mock trials that introduce legal concepts and vocabulary and give students practice in advocacy. Some states conduct Mock Trial championships. Some are modeled on high school competition and use prepared case packets; in others, students create their own trials based on laws and procedures that they themselves invent.

There is no standard format for middle school Mock Trial competition. Bar associations and local and regional forensics leagues frequently sponsor Mock Trial events. Generally, the format is similar to high school, but with fewer restrictions and less complex cases.

LAW SCHOOL

American law students often participate in intramural and interscholastic Mock Trial or trial advocacy, frequently referred to as "Moot Court." Some Moot Court competitions use criminal cases, and their format is similar to collegiate competition. Other competitions, including major intramural contests (such as the Ames competition at Harvard Law School) and the national championship sponsored by the American Mock Trial Association, use civil appellate cases. For Moot Court contests using civil litigation, teams typically consist of two or three attorneys on each side. Winners of major Moot Court competitions are frequently sought after for clerkships and other prestigious legal positions.

How the Mock Trial Proceeds

The Mock Trial begins when the judge enters the courtroom and instructs the jury regarding the facts of the case and applicable points of law. If either side has a pretrial motion, the judge and jury hear brief speeches from the prosecution and defense about those motions. The prosecution or plaintiff then gives an opening statement, which is followed by the opening statement of the defense. After the opening statements, examination of the witnesses begins. The prosecution calls its witnesses first and conducts a direct examination. When this is completed, the defense may cross-examine the witnesses. After the cross-examination, prosecution may offer additional questions, known as "redirect"; likewise, the defense may offer more questions, known as a "recross." This process is repeated for the two remaining prosecution witnesses. Once the prosecution has finished presenting witnesses, it rests its case; the process is repeated with the defense witnesses, having the defense attorneys direct and the prosecution attorneys cross-examine.

After all the witnesses have been examined, the trial moves to closing arguments. The prosecutor again goes first. After the defense finishes its closing argument, the prosecution may give a rebuttal argument if it has time remaining. In some competitions, the rebuttal is limited to the scope of the defense's closing arguments.

Judging

A Mock Trial judge has two responsibilities: reaching a verdict in the case and scoring the attorneys' and witnesses' presentations, generally on a 1–10 scale. The verdict and the scoring are independent judgments. The team with the highest total number of points wins the round. That team is often, but not always, the team that wins the judge's verdict. Given this method of scoring, it is possible for the defendant to be found guilty or lose the case, but for the defense team to still win the round.

In some competitions, points can be deducted from a team's score for testifying with information outside the scope of the Mock Trial materials and for unsportsmanlike conduct or abuse of objections.

When panels of judges are used, several different scoring protocols are employed. In one, the judges scoring the Mock Trial consist of the presiding judge and two scoring judges—all of whom score the teams. A second method has two scoring judges, with a presiding judge—but the presiding judge does not score the teams; rather, the judge simply votes or casts a ballot for one team or another. Yet another method of judging has three scoring judges—here, the presiding judge is not involved in the scoring of the teams. College invitationals often have two scoring judges, one of whom doubles as the presiding judge.

Australia and Asia

Australian high school Mock Trial competitions are held regionally and are sponsored by state and regional legal organizations. Schools field six-person teams: two barristers, one solicitor, two witnesses, and one court officer or magistrate's clerk. A magistrate, usually a member of the local legal community, delivers a verdict and rates each team member on a 1–10 scale. Teams are scheduled in individual contests against other teams approximately every three weeks, with different cases for each contest. After the first four rounds of competition, the strongest teams advance to an elimination bracket.

Secondary school Mock Trial competition is also popular in Asia, particularly in India and South Korea. Competitions are usually sponsored by bar organizations or law firms. International competitions between Australian and Asian or U.K. teams are also prominent.

United Kingdom

The Bar National Mock Trial Competition is an event for U.K. secondary school students. Students assume the roles of barristers and witnesses and present their case against teams from other schools. Other team members play the roles of court clerks and jurors. Several thousand students compete in regional contests each year. Regional competitions consist of three rounds. In two rounds, each team will alternately prosecute and defend one case; in the third round, each team will prosecute or defend a different case. The two teams with the highest scores go on to a fourth trial to decide the regional winning team, which then goes on to compete in the national final competition.

These Mock Trial performances are judged by circuit judges, recorders (sheriffs in Scotland), and senior barristers or advocates; they are held in Crown Courts across the U.K. (High Courts in Scotland).

PARLIAMENTARY DEBATE

Overview

Parliamentary Debate (or "parli") is very popular throughout the English-speaking world. Hundreds of colleges and universities in the United States, Canada, Great Britain, and more than 30 other nations participate in Parliamentary Debate. Parliamentary Debate is also the fastest-growing form of intercollegiate debate in the world.

Parliamentary Debate is very loosely based on the traditions of the U.K. House of Commons. Two sides (Government/Proposition/Affirmative and Opposition/Negative) debate a resolution, with speeches alternating between sides. Debaters offer points of information (POIs) similar to interruptions members of Parliament make in the House of Commons. Most parliamentary formats emphasize quick thinking and broad general knowledge rather than research and specialized knowledge, as debaters often have little or no preparation time once the topic has been announced.

In Parliamentary Debate, a different resolution is debated in each round. Resolutions are chosen from a wide variety of political, philosophical, economic, cultural, and humorous topics; debaters often have a broad scope in which to define the specific case for debate, which is drawn from the resolution.

Parliamentary Debate restricts the use of evidence. Published information (dictionaries, magazines, books, paper, or virtual files of articles) that participants may have consulted before the debate cannot be brought into the room in which the debate is held. Briefs of prepared arguments also may not be brought into the room. Debaters may refer only to any information that is within the realm of knowledge of liberally educated and informed citizens.

Parliamentary Debate has many variations, with distinct styles and slightly different structures. Among the most popular variations are American Parliamentary Debate, American High School Parliamentary Debate, Asian Parliamentary Debate, and Canadian Parliamentary Debate.

American Parliamentary Debate

American Parliamentary is an extemporaneous, generally policy-oriented form of two-person debate that values adaption for each audience. Debater role names are borrowed from the British Parliament. The speakers for the Proposition (or Government) are called the "prime minister" and "member of Government"; the speakers for the Opposition are called the "leader of the Opposition" and the "member of the Opposition." The judge is referred to as the "speaker."

Associations

Most American Parliamentary Debate teams belong to one of two associations: the American Parliamentary

Debate Association (APDA) and the National Parliamentary Debate Association (NPDA), each with distinct styles and rules.

AMERICAN PARLIAMENTARY DEBATE ASSOCIATION

The American Parliamentary Debate Association is the oldest parliamentary organization in the United States. Most of its member schools are located in the eastern United States. Although occasionally the tournament announces a topic 15 minutes in advance, in most APDA rounds the topic is proposed by the Government team.

Since the Opposition team arrives at the round with no prior knowledge of the case, to ensure a fair debate, some kinds of resolutions are not permitted. If the Opposition feels that the round fits any one of these categories, they may point this out during the leader's speech. If the judge agrees, Opposition wins. The five types of disallowed resolutions are:

- tight cases or resolutions. These are too one-sided to be debatable. For example, the Opposition team has little ground if the Government presents "racism is bad" as the resolution.

- truisms. These are arguments that are not disputable. "Barack Obama was the greatest Democratic president of the U.S. since Bill Clinton" is not debatable—the U.S. has had no other Democratic presidents since Bill Clinton.

- tautologies. Arguments that repeat the same thought but use different words. For example, "Good citizens should help the poor"—with goodness defined as "a willingness to do charitable acts"—is a circular resolution; the negative has no ground here.

- status quo resolutions. These support the current situation. ("The United States should have jury trials"); APDA assumes that, in a policy debate round, the Government should advocate change.

- specific-knowledge cases. Cases that are unfair to the Opposition because they require highly obscure knowledge to oppose effectively ("NASA should replace the current sealant used on the space shuttle with hypoxynucleotide-C4598").

Aside from these five limitations, virtually any topic is fair game. Debaters may also present opp-choice cases, in which the Government offers the Opposition the chance to choose which side of a topic they wish to defend in the round. For instance, the Government might begin the round by stating the motion ("That this house would support continued sanctions against Iran.") and allow the Opposition to choose whether they would rather support the motion (effectively becoming the Government, in that round) or opposing it.

Types of Arguments

APDA's format allows for a wide variety of cases, including (but not limited to): public policy, foreign policy, political theory, law and legal theory, moral hypotheticals, abstract philosophy, and time-space hypotheticals (which place the speaker in the position of a real-life, fictional, or historical figure). Occasionally, teams will choose to debate comedy cases; here, the round often becomes a contest of wit and style rather than pure analysis.

A time-space hypothetical resolution places the speaker in the position of some real-life, fictional, or historical figure. Only information accessible to a person in that position may be used in this type of round. For instance, "You are Socrates. Don't commit suicide" could not reference events that took place after Socrates' death. The speaker could also be a fictional character ("You are Homer Simpson. Do not sell your soul"), or a historical figure ("You are Abraham Lincoln. Do not sign the Emancipation Proclamation"), or virtually any other sentient individual.

APDA style is less structured, theoretical, and research-based than the NPDA style and demands less use of technical debate formalisms. On the other hand, it places a premium on creativity and quick response. APDA debates, like British Parliamentary Debates, emphasize slower, more oratorical speaking intended for a general audience.

NATIONAL PARLIAMENTARY DEBATE ASSOCIATION

The National Parliamentary Debate Association is the largest parliamentary organization in the United States. NPDA-style tournaments generally announce topics 15 minutes before each round (a few tournaments announce topic areas weeks in advance of the tournament). The topics are usually questions of policy, calling upon a government to take a specific course of action. NPDA teams conduct detailed research on a broad range of specific topics and prepare detailed arguments that resemble those found in American Policy Debate. Although the actual quotation of evidence is banned, NPDA is very much a research-based activity. The use of counterplans, disadvantages, and procedural arguments is increasingly common, and the average rate of delivery is much faster than in other parliamentary formats.

NPDA debate shares speaker order, speaking time, and other protocols with APDA debate, but is strikingly different in other ways. NPDA centers on current affairs; the philosophical, abstract, and whimsical topics often found in APDA are absent in NPDA. Although both associations have members throughout the United States, APDA schools are concentrated in the eastern United States, with NPDA schools more likely to be found in the western United States.

Structure

An American Parliamentary Debate round consists of six speeches, as follows:

Speaker	Time
Prime Minister Constructive (PMC)	7 minutes
Leader of Opposition Constructive (LOC)	8 minutes
Member of Government Constructive (MGC)	8 minutes
Member of Opposition Constructive (MOC)	8 minutes
Leader of Opposition Rebuttal (LOR)	4 minutes
Prime Minister Rebuttal (PMR)	5 minutes

There is no formal cross-examination or questioning period. Instead, debaters may raise parliamentary points during an opponent's speech, including points of information, points of order, and points of personal privilege. Points of order and points of personal privilege are serious charges and are raised only when a team has been genuinely abusive. Judges may penalize frivolous or excessive use of these objections.

Judging

A judge listens to the round and provides quantitative and qualitative assessments of the round as a whole and of the individual speakers. The judge decides which team has won the round and awards quality points to each speaker. Some rounds, especially elimination rounds, use a panel of judges. Judges are usually coaches or debaters themselves, but non-debater judges or lay judges are sometimes used.

American High School Parliamentary Debate

American High School Parliamentary Debate emphasizes broad knowledge, speaking skills, and an ability to organize arguments on a topic with very limited preparation time. This format is less widespread than policy, Lincoln–Douglas, or Public Forum, but is popular in public and private schools in California and Oregon and in private schools throughout the northeastern United States. High school formats are similar to collegiate National Parliamentary Debate Association formats. Topics, which are usually resolutions of policy of value, change each round, and are presented to the debaters 15–30 minutes before the round begins. Although speaking times vary slightly from circuit to circuit, they are very similar to APDA and NPDA speaking times. Points of information are common. Occasionally American high school parliamentary teams will compete against Canadian high school parliamentary teams. Home school leagues also promote varieties of Parliamentary Debate, and a number of college-sponsored summer programs teach Parliamentary Debate to high school students.

Asian Parliamentary Debate

Asian Parliamentary Debate (Asians) is possibly the most widely used format in the world. It is the predominant high school and college debate format in Australia and in many Asian countries. An affirmative team (sometimes called "Government" or "Proposition") defends a policy resolution; a negative team (sometimes called "Opposition") opposes it. Asian Parliamentary Debate is very straightforward, with few rules except that the Opposition cannot take a straight negative approach to disprove the Government's benefits. The Opposition must demonstrate that their position has a net benefit or fewer harms than the Government proposal. The absence of complicated rules enables speakers to take a wide range of approaches.

Topic Selection

The teams debating in a round are given three topics from which to choose and asked to rank them. The topics ranked third are discarded. If both teams rank the same topic first, it will be debated. If the teams rank the remaining two topics in reverse order, a flip of a coin will determine which will be debated. Occasionally tournaments will use a "secret topic" procedure, in which the sides and topics are revealed only an hour before the debate.

Structure

In Asians, each team has three members who are assigned the side they will debate.

The speaking order is as follows:

1. Prime Minister

2. Leader of the Opposition

3. Deputy Prime Minister

4. Deputy Leader of the Opposition

5. Government Whip

6. Opposition Whip

7. Opposition Reply Speech (can be delivered by either the 1st or 2nd Opposition speaker)

8. Government Reply Speech (can be delivered by either the 1st or 2nd Government speaker)

The prime minister begins by presenting the affirmative's interpretation of the resolution. She addresses the philosophical questions inherent in the resolution, offers arguments for adopting the resolution, and presents a model, or plan, for solving the problem that the resolution addresses. This speaker will also inform the judge of the "team split"—how the first two debaters expect to divide their labor. The leader of the Opposition then makes introductory remarks similar to those made by the prime minister, informs the judge of the negative "team split," and presents the negative's major arguments against the resolution, which may or may not include a "counter-model," or negative proposal.

The deputy prime minister refutes the arguments presented by the leader of the Opposition and advances the affirmative's arguments. This speaker may introduce new arguments. The speaker uses about half the time for refutation and the other half advancing her own case. The deputy leader of the Opposition has duties similar to the deputy prime minister.

The Government and Opposition whips refute opposing arguments and also summarize and synthesize the cases presented by their teams. Third speakers avoid minor or technical points, instead concentrating on broad, philosophical themes. New arguments are not permitted in these speeches.

At some tournaments, teams may present a reply speech during which each team compares the strengths and weaknesses of both cases. The Opposition usually makes their reply speech first. Usually only the first or second speaker of a team may make the reply speech. The goal of the reply speeches is to give a biased judgment about why the adjudicators should give their team the win.

As in other parliamentary formats, POIs are encouraged. The first and last minute of constructive speeches are protected time in which POIs are not allowed. Nor are POIs permitted during reply speeches.

Asians has no universally adopted speaking times. In Australia, high school speaking time limits correlate to the age and experience level of the debaters—sixth graders, for instance, might give 3-minute speeches, while high school seniors might have 8- or 9-minute time limits.

Debates where teams have less than a day to prepare are called "short preparation" or "impromptu" debates. In these particular formats, the tournament may require debaters to use only specific articles or sources in their preparation. In the event of restricted materials, the speaking times may be shortened.

Judging

Judging is usually done by a panel of three adjudicators who determine the winner by secret ballot rather than by consensus. Judges do not confer with one another before voting. The presiding judge will explain the panel's decision; should a dissenting judge wish, he or she can explain her perspective as well. Speakers are scored according to three categories: matter, manner, and method. Although scoring matrices vary, a 100-point scale is generally used, with 40 points each allocated to matter and manner and 20 points allocated to method. Points for the reply speeches are worth only half of the points scored in the substantive speeches. The team with the most total points is the winner.

Canadian Parliamentary Debate

Canadian Parliamentary Debate is an impromptu style that emphasizes argumentation and rhetoric rather than in-depth research. Debate involves two teams—the Government and the Opposition—each of which has two debaters. The members of the Government team are called the "prime minister" and the "minister of the Crown"; members of the Opposition are the "leader of the Opposition" and the "member of the Opposition." A speaker of the House is responsible for moderating the round and maintaining order. The teams alternate between Government and Opposition at tournaments.

Topic Selection

Most tournaments offer resolutions that are open to broad interpretation or allow the Government team to pick a topic and propose a case. Few restrictions are placed on the topic, except that it must be fairly debatable by both sides. Tight cases (those that leave the Opposition little room for argument) and topics requiring specialized knowledge are not permitted.

Structure

The speaking times at most Canadian tournaments are:

Prime Minister (Constructive)	7 minutes
Member of the Opposition	7 minutes
Minister of the Crown	7 minutes
Leader of the Opposition	10 minutes
Prime Minister (Rebuttal)	3 minutes

The prime minister constructive lays out the topic for debate and presents arguments in favor of their position. The Opposition team must then immediately present opposing arguments. New arguments can be presented in the first four speeches; they are prohibited in the rebuttal speeches.

Points of information are encouraged but can be offered only during unprotected time. The first and last minutes of constructed speeches are protected; rebuttal speeches are all protected. In a 10-minute leader of the Opposition speech, which combines constructive and rebuttal, the first minute and the last 4 minutes are protected. (Essentially, the format is protecting the first and last minutes of the constructive and the entire rebuttal portion of the speech.)

Variations

This standard format has two potential variations. One, the Prime Minister's Rebuttal Extension (PMRE), shaves a minute off the prime minister's constructive speech and adds a minute to the prime minister's rebuttal. If the PMRE variation is used, the first and last 30 seconds of the prime minister's constructive speech are protected time during which no POIs may be offered. The PMRE was designed to help compensate for the alleged inherent advantage to the Opposition.

The other variation, the split rebuttal, equalizes the time between the two Opposition speakers and reverses their speaking order. This adjustment of time limits leaves 3 minutes for the leader of the Opposition to deliver a rebuttal, which occurs immediately after the member of Opposition's speech. A split variation looks like this:

Prime Minister (Constructive)	7 minutes
Leader of the Opposition	7 minutes
Minister of the Crown	7 minutes
Member of the Opposition	7 minutes
Leader of the Opposition (Rebuttal)	3 minutes
Prime Minister (Rebuttal)	3 minutes

Before a round, a judge first asks the Government whether they want a PMRE; if they decline, the judge asks the

Opposition whether they want a split rebuttal. Once a team has decided, they cannot change their minds.

Delivery and Style

Canadian Parliamentary Debate is very much like British Parliamentary Debate. Speeches are delivered at conversational speed, and are intended for a general audience. Complex or technical arguments are seldom rewarded. Judges value wit and rhetoric as well as substantive analysis.

Judging

Judging is conducted either by a single judge or a panel. If a panel is used, members fill out their ballots independently without consulting each other.

PUBLIC FORUM DEBATE

Overview

Public Forum Debate (sometimes called "PF," "PuFo," or "PoFo") was invented by the National Forensic League in 2002. In Public Forum Debate, two-person teams, designated "pro" and "con," argue for or against a proposition of policy or value. Topics change each month and are informed by current events.

Public Forum Debates are designed for general audiences. In contrast to American Policy Debate, there is little focus on extreme speed, arcane debate jargon, or argumentation theory; instead, successful Public Forum debaters must make persuasive and logical arguments in a manner that is accessible to a wide variety of audiences. The debaters research the topic and present evidence to support their arguments, but good speaking, the use of rhetoric, and clear organization are emphasized.

Beginners can learn Public Forum relatively quickly. It has few specialized terms or concepts, and the topics require far less research than do American Policy or Lincoln–Douglas debate. Similarly, teachers with no prior debate background can learn to teach and coach Public Forum Debate relatively quickly. Clearly, Public Forum is a useful and accessible complement to other speech and debate events.

History

Beginning in the 1970s, many traditional debate educators became alienated from American Policy Debate. Common complaints included the rate of speech delivered, the complexity of arguments, the use of counterintuitive argument (e.g., that all advantages and disadvantages ended in nuclear war), and the extensive use of debate jargon. These complaints persisted, with participation in Policy Debate declining in the 1980s and 1990s. Although Lincoln–Douglas Debate was designed as an alternative to the excesses of Policy Debate, its delivery also became faster and its arguments more technical. In 2001, the National Forensic League (NFL) Executive Council began considering a new Policy Debate event. Council members Donus Roberts and Ted Belch were charged with drafting the model for an event called "Controversy," which became a NFL event during the 2002–2003 season. For 2003–2004 and 2004–2005, the event was called "Ted Turner Debate" (named after the communications entrepreneur). Subsequently, it was named "Public Forum Debate."

Public Forum Debate has grown rapidly. State leagues and invitational tournaments quickly adopted the event. The National Catholic Forensic League tournament and the Tournament of Champions both added Public Forum in 2007. By 2014, at least 20 different summer debate workshops offered instruction in Public Forum Debate.

Topic Selection

Public Forum topic selection is governed by the National Speech and Debate Association (NSDA), the successor to the National Forensic League. Originally, NSDA presented a new topic each month. In 2013, the executive council decided to begin the school year with a two-month topic (September–October) as a means of introducing Public Forum Debate to new students. Currently, it offers eight topics each year: September–October, November, December, January, February, March, April, and the national tournament topic. Any coach or debater may submit proposed topic areas or topics. A committee of senior debate educators, appointed by the NSDA executive director, meets each summer at the national tournament to discuss possible topic areas (for example, the Middle East or education policy). Because Public Forum Debate requires topics of very current interest, specific resolutions are never framed very far in advance. The committee conducts phone meetings each month to discuss topic areas and wording; they then announce a topic area and put two possible resolutions up to a vote by NSDA member schools. Voting begins about six weeks before a topic would take effect, and the resolution is announced a month in advance. For instance, voting on the November resolution would begin about September 20, with the resolution being announced on October 1.

Past resolutions include:

- Resolved: Single-gender classrooms would improve the quality of education in American public schools.

- Resolved: Immigration reform should include a path to citizenship for undocumented immigrants currently living in the United States.

- Resolved: The benefits of domestic surveillance by the National Security Agency (NSA) outweigh the harms.

- Resolved: Unilateral military force by the United States is justified to prevent nuclear proliferation.

- Resolved: Current U.S. foreign policy in the Middle East undermines our national security.

- Resolved: The main goal of U.S. public education should be to eliminate racial and economic achievement gaps.

Structure

Public Forum is unique among debate formats in that a coin flip determines the sides each team will argue. The winner of the flip may choose the side (pro or con) or the sequence (speaking first or last) that they prefer. The loser of the flip then makes the remaining choice. Thus, the negative team may begin the debate. Both teams and speakers alternate speeches until the conclusion of the debate.

A Public Forum Debate proceeds as follows:

Speech/Crossfire Period	Team/Speaker	Time
Constructive Speech	Team A: First Speaker	4 minutes
Constructive Speech	Team B: First Speaker	4 minutes
1st Crossfire	Team A: First Speaker and Team B: First Speaker	3 minutes

Rebuttal Speech	Team A: Second Speaker	4 minutes
Rebuttal Speech	Team B: Second Speaker	4 minutes
2nd Crossfire	Team A: Second Speaker and Team B: Second Speaker	3 minutes
Summary Speech	Team A: First Speaker	2 minutes
Summary Speech	Team B: First Speaker	2 minutes
Grand Crossfire	All Speakers	3 minutes
Final Focus	Team A: Second Speaker	2 minutes
Final Focus	Team B: Second Speaker	2 minutes

Constructive speeches begin with a brief introduction, followed by definition or clarification of key terms in the resolution. Some teams may also offer brief framework observations, suggesting criteria that the judge might use to decide the round. ("The team that best protects the rights of citizens should win the round." "The judge should value empirical evidence from the past and present over predictions of what might happen in the future.") These observations are followed by two to four major arguments, or contentions, supporting the pro or con side of the resolution. The constructive speeches are completely prewritten and do not include direct refutation of an opponent's case.

A crossfire period follows the two constructive speeches. Public Forum crossfire differs from cross-examination periods in policy and Lincoln–Douglas in that the two speakers take turns questioning each other; informal give-and-take is permitted. Usually the debater who has not just spoken asks the first question. Public Forum debaters use crossfire to clarify points, to call attention to the absence or inadequacy of supporting evidence, to point out contradictions or tension between opponents' arguments, or simply to highlight the weakness of an opponent's argument.

After crossfire, the first team's second speaker gives a 4-minute rebuttal speech, attacking the second team's observations and contentions point by point. The speaker may attack his opponent's logic, criticize his opponent's examples or evidence, explain how his own case answers his opponent's cases, and provide evidence contradicting his opponent's claims. The second team's rebuttalist will attack the first team's case but may reserve 60–90 seconds to defend her own case against the attacks of the first rebuttalist. Following another crossfire, the first speakers on each team then present 2-minute summary speeches. These speeches are half the length of the constructive and rebuttal speeches, so it is not possible to refute all opposing arguments; the speakers must begin the process of choosing the arguments that are likely to win them the debate. The first summary speaker will spend some time answering specific arguments made in her opponent's rebuttal before summarizing the most important arguments; the second summary speaker can spend all of her 2 minutes emphasizing critical points.

The summary speeches are followed by grand crossfire in which all four speakers participate. Judges expect that grand crossfire will be quick and lively, with speakers often interrupting and even talking over one another, though judges may penalize bullying or overt rudeness.

The final focus speeches often determine the judge's decision in a closely contested round. Again, the debaters cannot talk about every issue in the round; they must choose their arguments carefully and provide a framework for the judge's decision. This allows the judge to hear which arguments/evidence each team views as the most important to his or her case; it also summarizes the entire debate. Often a final focus speaker will apply a specific organizational pattern. Some examples include:

- The "world of the pro" versus the "world of the con"—demonstrating the difference between a society that has adopted the resolution (created stronger gun control, for example) versus the status quo.

- Comparing the strongest individual arguments of each team and demonstrating why his side's argument is more persuasive.

- Identifying two, or perhaps three, reasons why the pro or con team wins the round.

New arguments are not permitted in final focus; extensions of arguments developed in previous speeches are allowed.

Each team also has a total of 2 minutes of preparation time that they can use before any of their speeches. For instance, a team might choose to take 30 seconds of prep time before their rebuttal speech; that would leave 90 seconds for use before the summary and/or final focus. Often the debaters keep time for themselves, though the judge may also act as timekeeper.

Evidence

Public Forum debaters, like policy and Lincoln–Douglas debaters, use statistics and quotations from experts as evidence to support their arguments. Unlike debaters in some other formats, they do not always quote published evidence word-for-word; very often, they simply paraphrase or refer to an article or book, with the understanding that they can make the original text of the evidence available to opponents or to a judge. Public Forum debaters are also more likely to use simple analogies, historical precedent, or commonly known facts as support for claims. The paraphrase of evidence in Public Forum has become controversial; many coaches are concerned that the practice encourages misrepresentation or outright fabrication of evidence. Several task forces, including a recently formed NSDA committee, are addressing evidence issues, with the hope that some uniform code of evidence presentation might be agreed upon.

Delivery and Style

Compared with policy or even Lincoln–Douglas rounds, Public Forum Debate is quite formal. Suits and ties are standard dress for boys; girls wear skirts or business suits. The debaters seldom, if ever, interrupt or prompt each other during speaking time. The first two speakers often include formal words of introduction ("Good morning. My name is _____, and I am the first pro speaker, defending the resolution _____."). Crossfire is conducted standing, with both debaters facing the judge. Grand crossfire, on the other hand, is conducted with all four debaters seated, if possible, around a table where they can all speak directly to one another.

Common Arguments

Public Forum topics always concern the desirability of a course of action; debaters' arguments, accordingly, focus on the advantages and disadvantages of that action. The resolutions do not usually contain an actor (e.g., "the U.S. federal government should . . . "), and NSDA rules specifically state that teams should defend the resolution as a general statement and should not offer plans or counterplans. Time constraints and the nature of the judging pool preclude the use of complex, multi-step arguments like policy disadvantages. Although values or ethical/philosophical arguments are sometimes made in Public Forum, rounds usually center on a utilitarian framework. (On a gun control topic: Would stricter gun laws reduce violent crime? Can such laws be enforced or would they simply create a new black market for weapons? Are current laws sufficient if properly enforced?)

Debate theory arguments are rarely presented. Teams may, on occasion, argue that an opponent is unfairly interpreting a term of the resolution or that their examples are atypical or unrepresentative and should be disregarded.

Questions of fairness or abuse are rarely central to any Public Forum round, however.

Special Features

The Public Forum format has two unique elements. Unlike other debate formats, a coin flip determines the side and order each team will argue. The coin flip format also makes it possible for a team to debate most or even all of its rounds on one side of the resolution, whereas policy, Parliamentary, and Lincoln–Douglas tournaments make certain that teams debate an equal number of affirmative and negative rounds. Most states use this format, and it is used at all NSDA district qualifying tournaments, at NSDA Nationals and at the Tournament of Champions. Some states (California, Minnesota, and others) and leagues (the National Catholic Forensic League) deviate from the NSDA model and mandate that the pro team always speak first.

The format also mandates three crossfire periods during which participants may both ask and answer questions in an informal give-and-take. The first two crossfire periods involve one speaker from each team; the third crossfire period, also called "grand crossfire," involves all four debaters.

Judging

A Public Forum Debate tournament consists of a number of preliminary rounds of competition, usually followed by elimination rounds—a series of "sudden death" competitions for teams who performed best in preliminary rounds. These continue until two remaining teams compete in a final round. Generally single judges decide the outcome of preliminary rounds, while panels of judges (three, five, or seven) decide elimination rounds.

The judge acts as a disinterested observer who has consciously cast aside his own opinions and preconceptions regarding the debaters' arguments. He must select a winner based on the arguments and evidence that are actually presented in the round. To choose a winner, a judge must evaluate each line of argument in detail and ultimately determine whether the resolution is a good idea.

The creators of Public Forum Debate assumed that debates would take place before community or lay judges. Some Public Forum judges are debate coaches or former debaters, but most are still persons with no particular expertise in debate; very often, the parents of debaters are recruited to judge contests. Judges may or may not take notes, and they are unlikely to accept complex or counterintuitive arguments. Because many tournaments do not permit judges to examine evidence after the round, debaters' explanation of evidence is crucial.

In addition to determining which team won the debate, the judge must award speaker points to each competitor. The decision and the awarding of points are largely independent processes. Speaker points are a more subjective evaluation of each debater's skills. Speaker point formulas vary throughout local state and regional organizations. Most tournaments use values ranging from 0 to 30. In practice, points below 25 are reserved for extremely poor performances, while a perfect score of 30 is rare and warranted only by a truly outstanding performance. Generally, speaker points are seen as less important than wins and losses. Judges may, and sometimes do, give fewer speaker points to the winning team than to the losing team. Most tournaments also present debaters with speaker awards—recognition for debaters who received the highest point totals in the tournament.

WORLD SCHOOLS STYLE DEBATE

Overview

World Schools (Worlds) was "purpose built" for the first World Schools Debating Championship in 1988. Originally designed to be a format different from those of all other national competitions, it subsequently became popular worldwide and is now used at both national and regional competitions.

World Schools asks speakers to grapple with general issues rather than specific programs or proposals. Speakers are encouraged to address the broad themes that surround topics rather than focus on details of implementation or political expediency. Overall, this format rewards good teamwork, preparation, participation, and persuasion. The debate is between teams, not individuals. Each speaker has a role in presenting the team's case and also attacking the other side while defending her own arguments. The format encourages the use of points of information (POIs) to keep debaters involved when they are not speaking. World Schools marks debaters for content, style, and strategy; thus, a debater must be aware of not just what she says but how she says it.

History

University debaters have competed internationally since the early twentieth century, but international secondary school debating was rare until the 1980s. The first Worlds tournament for secondary schools was sponsored by the Australian Debate Federation in 1988; it was held in conjunction with the Worlds Universities Championships, which were held in Sydney that year. A second World Schools championship was held in Canada in 1990, and the tournament has been held annually ever since.

Topic Selection

Some Worlds tournaments announce topics (or motions) before the tournament, but most tournaments use a mix of limited-preparation topics (announced 15–45 minutes in advance) and impromptu topics (announced by the tournament or presented by the proposition team at the beginning of the round). At the World Schools championships, topics are prepared by a committee whose members reflect the diversity of the teams in attendance. The topics may be either propositions of fact (testing the truth of a statement), propositions of policy (calling for government or international organization action), or propositions of value (calling on the House to prefer one principle or quality over another), though recent topics have been preponderantly propositions of policy.

Examples of Worlds topics include:

- This House believes that affluent nations should accept more refugees.

- This House disapproves of cloning.

- This House refuses to negotiate with terrorists.

- This House believes that Turkey is better off outside the European Union.

Structure

In World Schools, six individuals speak during each debate: three for the proposition and three for the opposition. The debate comprises eight parts.

A contemporary World Schools debate proceeds as follows:

Speaker	Time
1. First Proposition	8 minutes
2. First Opposition	8 minutes
3. Second Proposition	8 minutes
4. Second Opposition	8 minutes
5. Third Proposition	8 minutes
6. Third Opposition	8 minutes
7. Opposition Reply Speech (can be delivered by either the 1st or 2nd opposition speaker)	4 minutes

8. Proposition Reply Speech	4 minutes

(can be delivered by either the 1st or 2nd proposition speaker)

During the first six speeches, debaters present substantive arguments and rebut the arguments of the other team. As the debate progresses, speakers move from presenting new arguments and issues to addressing issues already raised.

The first speaker for the proposition defines the motion and presents the proposition's case, which may include a proposed plan of action (if the motion is a proposition of policy). The first speaker for the opposition refutes the arguments offered by the proposition. The speaker may simply argue that the proposition's arguments fail on their own terms—they are illogical or lack proper support through evidence and example. She may offer counter-examples or counterevidence, attempting to disprove the proposition's arguments. She may also offer a counter-case, an alternative course of action that might solve the problem the motion addresses. The first speaker for the opposition may also challenge the proposition's definition or interpretation of the motion.

The second speaker for the proposition answers the refutation provided by the first opposition speaker; he may also introduce additional arguments supporting the motion. The second speaker for the opposition answers the second speaker for the proposition and may introduce additional arguments opposing the motion.

The third speakers filter out less important arguments, answer the second speakers on the most important arguments, and rebuild the logic and structure of their case or position. Reply speakers isolate one or two critical points in the debate, explain why those points are, in fact, critical, and explain why winning those points wins the round for their side.

Each team finishes with a reply speech in which the speakers summarize the key points of both sides, emphasize the areas of clash, and analyze the debate to show the adjudicators that their team has won. Either the first or second speaker may give his team's reply speech. Note that the order of speeches is reversed at this point in the debate, so that the proposition team, which had the first word, will also have the last word. Additionally, no new arguments may be introduced in the reply speeches.

Debaters engage each other using points of information during the first six speeches. The first and last minute of each speech are "protected time," meaning that no points of information may be offered.

Some competitions permit only 5 or 6 minutes for main speeches and 3 minutes for reply speeches. Other tournaments offer a 2-minute break before the reply speeches to allow team members to confer with one another.

Delivery and Style

World Schools Debate is judged on three elements: matter (content), manner (style), and strategy. Although each of these elements is judged separately, to be successful, a debater must combine them. Thus, a debater must present sound arguments in a logical manner and with an interesting, persuasive speaking style. A good speaker makes the substance of what she says integral to how she says it, using an appropriate style for the matter at hand.

Judging

World Schools judges may be former debaters, debate coaches, or members of the community that hosts the tournament. Judges are asked to rate each of the first three speeches on a 0 to 100 scale; in practice, scores fall between 60 and 80. The shorter reply speeches are rated on a 0 to 50 scale. The World Schools Championship tournament advises judges to grade 40 percent on speaking style, 40 percent on quality of arguments, and 20 percent on strategy. If a round is heard by a panel of judges, each makes her own decision and does her own scoring; the panel then chooses one judge to announce the winner and make educational comments to both teams after the round has concluded.

ABBREVIATIONS & ACRONYMS

ad hom—ad hominem (or *argumentum ad hominem*)

ADS—after-dinner speaking

AFA—American Forensic Association

AGD—attention-getting device

APDA—American Parliamentary Debate Association

A-spec—agent specification

CEDA—Cross Examination Debate Association

cite—citation

CUSID—Canadian University Society for Intercollegiate Debate

DLO—deputy leader of the Opposition

DPM—deputy prime minister

ESU—English Speaking Union

EUDC—European Universities Debating Championship

extemp—extemporaneous speaking

flex prep—flex preparation

IDEA—International Debate Education Association

IPPF—International Public Policy Forum

I-spec—implementation specification

LO—leader of the Opposition

MG—member of the Government

MJP—mutual judge preferences

MO—member of the Opposition

NAUDL—National Association of Urban Debate Leagues

NCFCA—National Christian Forensics and Communication Association

NCFL—National Catholic Forensics League

NDT—National Debate Tournament

NEDA—National Educational Debate Association

NFA—National Forensic Association

NFL—National Forensic League

NITOC—National Invitational Tournament of Champions

NJFL—National Junior Forensic League

NorthAms—North American Debating Championship

NPDA—National Parliamentary Debate Association

NSDA—National Speech and Debate Association

O-spec—overspecification

OW—Opposition whip

PIC—plan inclusive counterplan

PM—prime minister

PMRE—Prime Minister's Rebuttal Extension

POI—point of information

RFD—reason for decision

RVI—reverse voting issue

spec case—specialized knowledge case

UADC—United Asian Debating Championships

UDL—Urban Debate Leagues

WIDPSC—World Individual Debating and Public Speaking Championships

WSDC—World Schools Debating Championships

WUDC—World Universities Debating Championship

THEMATIC INDEX

AMERICAN POLICY DEBATE
add-on
advantage
advantage counterplan
agent counterplan
agent specification (or A-spec)
alternative
alternative justification
attitudinal inherency
backflowing
best definition standard
blank slate judging
block
blow up
brink
business confidence disadvantage
card
case side
circumvention argument
closed cross-examination
comparative advantage
competing interpretations
conditional argument
consultation counterplan
counterplan
countervision
counterwarrant

criteria-goals case
cross-examination
cutting evidence
decision rule
disadvantage
discursive impact
dispositionality
division of labor
double turnaround
education standard
elections disadvantage
Emory switch
enabling planks
enforcement plank
evidence, piece of
example of the resolution
exclusion counterplan
existential inherency
extratopicality
fairness standard
fiat power
field context definition
first affirmative constructive
first affirmative rebuttal
first affirmative speaker
first negative constructive
first negative rebuttal
first negative speaker
frontline
functional competition
future abuse
games theory
generic argument

ground standard
harm
hypothesis testing
impact turnaround
implementation specification (I-spec)
inherency
in-round abuse
intellectual endorsement
intrinsicness
intrinsicness permutation
jurisdiction standard
justification argument
kickout
Kritik
legislative intent
linear impact
link turnaround
literature standard
minor repair
mutual exclusivity
need-plan case
negation theory
negative block
negative fiat
net benefits
normal means
object fiat
open cross examination
overspecification (O-spec)
permutation
plan
plan focus
plan inclusive counterplan

plan meet need
plan side
policy making
political capital disadvantage
politics disadvantage
post-fiat implication
predictability standard
pre-fiat implication
presumption
real world
reasonability
rebuttal speech
referendum counterplan
resolution
resolutional focus
reversibility
second affirmative
second negative
severance
severance permutation
solvency
solvency advocate
spending disadvantage
spike
status quo
stock issues
straight turn
structural inherency
study counterplan
tag
takeout
textual competition
time frame permutation

time suck
topicality
trade-off disadvantage
uniqueness
Urban Debate Leagues
whole resolution
word PIC
workability

ARGUMENTATION
ad hominem
analogy
analytic argument
argument
argument from authority
assertion
begging the question
causation
circular reasoning
claim
contention
correlation
deduction
enthymeme
fallacy
hasty generalization
induction
link
mitigation
naturalistic fallacy
non sequitur
post hoc ergo propter hoc
power matching

red herring
sign reasoning
straw man
syllogism
tautologies
Toulmin model
trusim
tu quoque
warrant

BRITISH PARLIAMENTARY DEBATE
deputy leader of the Opposition
deputy prime minister
European Universities Debating Championship
garden path
general knowledge standard
Government
Government whip
heckling
leader of the Opposition
member of the Government
member of the Opposition
motion
Opposition whip
point of clarification
point of information
point of order
point of personal privilege
prime minister
short diagonal

COMPETITION AND TOURNAMENTS
adjusted speaker points
after-dinner speaking
argument preference
ballot
blank slate judging
bracket
break round
breaking brackets
bye
chair
chief adjudicator
closed adjudication
closeout
community judge
community preferences
competing interpretations
critic-of-argument judging
debatability standard
declamation
disclosure of decisions
double entry
double octafinal round
dramatic interpretation
drop
duo interpretation
elimination round bracket
final round
flighting
flip
flip round
flow judge
high-low speaker points

hit
interpretive events
judge panels
junior varsity
lag pairing
lay judge
locked
low point win
maverick
mutual judge preferences
novice
octafinal round
open division
opposition wins
oral critique
preliminary round
preparation time
program oral interpretation
quarterfinal round
reason for decision
rhetorical criticism
role of the ballot
round
schematic
semifinal round
short preparation debates
skills judging
spar debates
speaker points
squirrel
strike
strike sheets
swing team

switch side
time limits
tournament
triple octafinal round
walkover
white copy

CONGRESSIONAL DEBATE
adjournment
agenda
amendment
appeal a decision of the chair
authorship speech
bill
call to order
chamber
committee
committee of the whole
Congressional questioning period
con speech
dilatory motion
divide a motion
division of the house
docket
floor
friendly question
gavel
geography
longest standing
null and void clause
resolved clause
whereas clause

FORENSICS

agent
artificial competition
bias
big picture
block
brainstorming
burden of proof
burden of rejoinder
card
case
citation
clash
closed-ended question
constructive speech
counterplan
coverage
cross-application
crystallization
data
debate
debate across the curriculum
debate workshop
decision calculus
definitions
dilemma
disclosure
discourse
dropped argument
empirically denied
evaluative argument
even if
evidence

extension
file
flashing
flip
flowing
forensics
framework
grouping
highlighting
impact
impact calculus
indicts
judging styles
line by line
loaded term
magnitude
mandate
middle school forensics
narrative
new argument
novice
observation
off-case arguments
on-case arguments
online debating
open-ended question
overview
paperless debate
political capital
preempt
prima facie case
procedural arguments
prompting

proposition
proposition of fact
proposition of policy
proposition of value
rebuttal
refutation
roadmap
role playing
sandbagging
scenario
shift
should
significance
signposting
specialized knowledge case
speed ballot
spreading
squirrel case
straight refutation
Stoa USA
theory arguments
time frame
topic selection
turnaround
unconditional argument
underview
uniqueness
value
voting issue
weighing

FORMATS
American High School Parliamentary Debate

American Parliamentary Debate
American Policy Debate
Asian Parliamentary Debate
British Parliamentary Debate
Canadian Parliamentary Debate
Chamber Debate
Congressional Debate
European Square Debate
Individual Events
Jes Debate
Karl Popper Debate
Lincoln–Douglas Debate
Mace Debate
Mock Trial
Moot Court
Paris-style debating
Parliamentary Debate
Public Forum Debate
World Schools Debate
Worlds Format debate
Worlds University Debate

INDIVIDUAL EVENTS

children's literature
communication analysis
declamation
dramatic interpretation
duo interpretation
expository speaking
extemporaneous commentary
extemporaneous debate
extemporaneous speaking
grace period

group discussion
humorous interpretation
impromptu speaking
informative speaking
limited preparation events
mixed interpretation
oratorical interpretation
original oratory
original poetry
pentathlon
persuasive speaking
platform events
poetry interpretation
program oral interpretation
prose interpretation
rhetorical criticism
speaking order
triathlon

KARL POPPER DEBATE
method of agreement
method of correlation
method of difference

LINCOLN-DOUGLAS DEBATE
a priori argument
cross-examination
flex preparation
ought
rebuttal speech
resolution
reverse voting issue

value criterion
value premise

MOCK TRIAL
affidavit
case packet
closing argument
cross-examination
defendant
direct examination
exhibit
prosecution
recross
redirect
statement of facts
stipulation

ORGANIZATIONS AND TOURNAMENTS
American Forensic Association
American Parliamentary Debate Association
Canadian University Society for Intercollegiate Debate
Cross Examination Debate Association
English Speaking Union
European Universities Debating Championship
International Debate Education Association
International Public Policy Forum
National Association of Urban Debate Leagues
National Catholic Forensics League
National Christian Forensics and Communication
    Association
National Debate Tournament
National Educational Debate Association

National Forensic Association
National Forensic League
National Invitational Tournament of Champions
National Junior Forensic League
National Parliamentary Debate Association
National Speech and Debate Association
North American Debating Championship
Pi Kappa Delta
United Asian Debating Championships
Urban Debate Leagues
World Individual Debating and Public Speaking
    Championships
World Schools Debating Championships
World Universities Debating Championship

PARLIAMENTARY DEBATE
Chamber Debate
comedy case (American)
counter-case (American)
counter-model
counterplan
dino (American)
equity officer
European Square Debate
floor vote
general knowledge standard
Government
grace period
hung case
iron man
Jes Debate
leader of the Opposition
literal motion

long diagonal
loose link
Mace Debate
manner
matter
member of the Government
member of the Opposition
metaphorical motion
method
model
motion
opp-choice case
Opposition
Paris-style debating
point of clarification
point of information
point of order
point of personal privilege
prime minister
Prime Minister's Rebuttal Extension
proposition
protected time
reply speech
secret topic debates
seeding
snug case
specialized knowledge case
squirrel
straight link
team split (Australia-Asia)
tight case (American)
tight link (American)
time-space case

United Asian Debating Championships

PUBLIC FORUM DEBATE
con team
crossfire
final focus
flex case
grand crossfire
rebuttal speech
resolution
summary speech
Ted Turner Debate

PUBLIC SPEAKING
attention device
audience adaptation
constraint
delivery
ethos
logos
pathos
performance
rhetoric
rhetorical situation
transitional movement
vocalized pause
warm ups
word economy

WORLDS FORMAT DEBATE
back-tabbing
chief adjudicator

closed adjudication
counteropp
iron man
long diagonal
manner
matter
panacea
reply speech
wing
World Schools Debate
Worlds format